One World. One Company.

How some of the best companies in the world are becoming global.
And why you should, too.

BY FREDRIK HÄRÉN

INTERESTING BOOKS
Copyright 2013 © Fredrik Härén, Singapore
ISBN 978-91-975471-0-9
www.interesting.org

DESIGNED BY André Wognum · www.wognum.se

To my lovely wife, Elaine,
and my precious son, Lucas.

You are the world to me.

Introduction

I want to begin with a couple of quotes from two top managers that I interviewed for this book. I asked them, *"What do you say to the people who say that the corporate world is not becoming more global?"*

One of them replied, *"I say that they are full of s***, and I believe that they have been living with their head in the sand the last few years."*

Another senior manager smiled and said, in a more gentle manner, *"In our world this is just not true. I can give you thousands of examples of how we are operating in a truly global business environment. And how we relocate our resources around the world according to where we think they will be the most profitable. We [now] look at the market on a global scale."*

This book is written specifically for business leaders, managers and employees of companies where the organization has realized how the world of business has changed and become more global.

The readers I target with this book are people who want to understand what this change will mean, and who want to know what they—as companies and as managers—need to do to adapt and change.

In a survey done around the theme of this book to the delegates of the Cannes Creative Festival, a vast majority of the respondents agreed that there had been increased competition from global companies in the last five years. At the same time, 100 percent of the respondents replied that they saw "increased global competition as an opportunity." I agree with this viewpoint. And so do all the people I have interviewed for this book.

Treat this book as an inspiration about this opportunity, and as guidance on how to seize it.

Why I wrote this book.
And why I wrote it now.

I wrote my first book in 1995. It was a book about this new thing called "the Internet," and how it would change the way companies would be run. It was one of the first books on Internet and business published in Sweden. I wrote that book because I had come to realize how the Internet was starting to change business, and because I could see how it would transform many industries in the near future.

I can still remember how most business people at the time thought that I was out of my mind. Today we talk about the "Digital Divide"—how some people saw new opportunities because they were able to understand how new digital technology, like the Internet, would transform our lives. Other people, and companies, did not understand the change that the digital revolution created and therefore lived in ignorance of its possibilities.

I wrote this book now, because I am feeling just like I did in 1994. I feel that some business people, and some companies, are truly grasping how changes in recent years have created a new landscape with new opportunities—while others live in ignorance of how the world has changed.

I call it the "Global Divide."

Some get it.

Some do not.

This is a book about the people and companies that do. And what we can learn from them.

FREDRIK HÄRÉN

Disclaimer

Writing a book about global companies is tricky. Some will tell you that this is nothing new—that it's been around since the Romans, or at least since Columbus. Others will tell you that the whole idea of "being global" is an over-hyped buzzword with little in common with how most people live their lives.

Both objections have some merit, though they aim their criticism from opposite viewpoints. Let's clarify why these objections miss their mark.

CRITICISM: "THIS HAS ALREADY HAPPENED."

Response:

There are literally hundreds of books on globalization, and many of them were written 20, 30 or even 40 years ago. So why a book on global companies now? Isn't this an old story?

This is not a book about globalization. It is a book about how companies, because of globalization (and other events), have started to become more global in the way they are run. How they went from being "international companies," to "MNCs" (Multi National Corporations)—and now to "TGCs" (Truly Global Companies).

It is this shift to Truly Global Companies that this book is about —a shift that has happened in the last three to seven years for most of the companies I have interviewed for this book.

For example: SKF was founded in 1907 and was an "international Swedish company" for about 100 years. According to its CEO, it was not until 2005 that they truly started to become a "global company." In their case, it was due in large part to the rapid growth of China. (Read more about SKF in the chapter "A Global Case Study".) For most large companies in the world, it is a shift that they have yet to make.

CRITICISM:
"THIS HAS NOT HAPPENED YET."

Response:

There are others who will argue that the world is not as global as some may think. (Actually there is a whole book, called "World 3.0," on that thesis.) Only seven percent of rice is exported. Close to 97% of the world's population is living in the same country they were born in, and so on.

But, again, this is not a book on globalization, at least not in the sense that most people think about globalization. It is not about jobs being "stolen" from one country to another. It is actually not about countries at all. It is about how some companies have been able to act as one company, everywhere.

Again, it is a book about global companies. Not a book about globalization.

If a Swedish-born media buyer lives and work as an consultant for a media agency in Sweden, giving advice to a local Swedish chain of hair salons on which local media to buy, then there is not a lot of that work that would be counted as being "global." But if she works for Mindshare, then she is also part of a global organization that is sharing best practices, news and information across its network of 113 offices in 82 countries. (Read more about Mindshare in the chapter "Share Your Mind…".)

Thus, companies can be more global than they seem.

How to use this book

The companies featured in this book are included because I think they have done something remarkable that others can learn from, when it comes to how to be a global organization. That does not mean that they do everything right. No company does everything right. No person is a saint, and no company is perfect. Actually, many of the companies in this book will readily, and honestly, concede that they have a long way to go before they are truly global companies. But they have embarked on the journey and, by doing so, have something to teach others.

Each chapter in this book features a different company and ends with the take away I personally found most interesting, refreshing or beneficial. While the companies I write about might be heading in the right direction toward being global companies, or have already arrived, they may also fail in other ways that I choose not to highlight. My purpose with the setup of this book is to provide a smorgasbord of different lessons revolving around the ways some of the best companies in the world are doing things correctly.

If you are looking for a simple list of "Ten-ways-to-become-a-global-company," you will be disappointed. This book revolves around real-life stories and examples of what others are doing. The conclusion of what you can learn from them and what you can take away is something that has to be part of your reading experience.

I am not a strong supporter of top ten lists or easy-to-remember abbreviations, but I am a strong believer in the power of example and the impact of stories.

As always, take the advice that makes the most sense to you, and discard what you find irrelevant, not applicable, or just plain wrong for you. Take the best from the best, and merge it with what you are doing right yourself.

Let's begin.

The first thing I want you to do is to write down a few words that come into your mind when you think about "TGCs" (Truly Global Companies).

What is a global company to you? Which company is the most global company you can think of? Why? How global is your company? How global are you?

_____

_____

_____

_____

_____

"One World, One Company" TOYOTA

One World. One Company.
About the title for this book.

SCENE: SLOVENIA, SINGAPORE & FRANKFURT

In September 2011, a couple of hundred employees of Deloitte Sweden flew to a hotel in the beautiful countryside of Slovenia for their yearly company conference. The theme of the conference was "As One."

Later that year, a couple of hundred sales representatives of HP Asia flew in to the massive Marina Bay Sands hotel and conference center in Singapore for their yearly company conference. The theme of their conference was "One Team, One Way. One Mission."

I was the keynote speaker at both conferences, which meant that I heard firsthand how these companies were preparing for the future. By 2012, the title for the book I was writing seemed obvious. The phrase, in one way or another, kept recurring.

BACKGROUND

Then in March 2012 I delivered a speech for a couple of hundred sales and marketing professionals of Sapa Profiles who had flown to conveniently located Frankfurt for their yearly company conference.

The theme of that conference was "One Sapa. One Sales and Marketing."

The change Sapa was in the middle of was, in many ways, a perfect example of the *"One World. One Company"* transition so many companies are trying to perform right now.

I had the opportunity to sit down with John Thuestad, President of Sapa Profiles, to talk about how Sapa was changing.

Sapa produces and sells aluminum profiles. Founded in 1963, for the longest time Sapa operated and thrived as a local European company. But in the last few years, something changed. When I asked Thuestad when the change occurred, he replied, "It started in 2003–2005, and intensified in 2009. Before that we did not act like a global company." And they didn't have to. Most business was local, with few customers wanting global contracts and the threat from cheap competition from Asia not yet an issue. Then everything changed at once.

"We saw that structural change in our customer base, and as the world changed, they wanted us to globalize with them," said Thuestad. Then he told me how some of their biggest customers, like IKEA, Ahlstrom and Siemens, began asking for global contracts.

If Sapa was able to piggyback on their customers' drive to become global, Sapa would be able to get large contracts from customers who were driving innovation and willing to pay a premium to a supplier able to deliver its products with consistent quality worldwide.

If Sapa was not able to keep up with this demand, they would find themselves cut off from substantial deals, left to compete with smaller local clients against low cost suppliers from Asia.

It was clear which of those two scenarios Sapa wanted to be part of. Thuestad looked me in the eyes to ensure I understood just how committed he and his company were to this change, and said, "We will move with our customers. Our ambition now is to be a global company."

Sapa is not there yet. Thuestad labels Sapa today as a "globally regional company." For many of their offices in Europe, just 10–15% of their business is from global contracts. But it is increasing, and in the cutthroat business of aluminum profile, those orders could be the difference between thriving and suffering. Sapa is not on a mission to become "One" because it is a nice thing to do. They are doing it to stay alive.

TAKE AWAY

The title of this book—*One World. One Company.*—was not chosen to be unique. It was chosen because the phrase, in slight variations, often and increasingly, has been used by companies trying to get their stakeholders to grasp the transition to global company that these organizations are trying to pull off.

Throughout this book I include some of the companies I observed using a variation of the *"One World. One Company."* slogan for internal or external use.

Like all slogans, the *"One World. One Company."* phrase can be mocked by cynics as empty corporate B.S. But, like all slogans, it can also be seen as a profound truth condensed into an easily communicated package.

I hope you will read the phrase—and this book—as it was intended: As an inspirational tale about how some companies and organizations are trying to transform themselves to better handle the challenges of a smaller, faster, more interconnected and interdependent business world.

Notes

"One World. One Company." NETWORK TELEPHONE SERVICES INC.

"Bad English:" A Good Idea
How a simple idea releases more power at Volvo Group.

SCENE: A RESORT OUTSIDE GOTHENBURG

A few years back I had the privilege to deliver a session on business creativity for the top management of Volvo Group. After the session I got to sit down for lunch with Leif Johansson, then the CEO of Volvo Group, to talk about how the company looked at running the company as one.

BACKGROUND

Volvo Group is a company that has realized the symbolic value that rules and regulations can play when a company is trying to become truly global. With about 100,000 employees, production facilities in 20 countries, and sales in more than 190 markets, this manufacturer of trucks, buses and construction equipment is a global company. They sell their products under more than ten different brands, including Volvo, Mack, Renault Trucks, Eicher, SDLG and so forth. Many may connect the different brands to different countries, but Volvo Group is focused on running the company as one global entity. They synchronize production between different brands to get economy of scale.

Leif Johansson told me how, inside the company, they half jokingly talk about the "official language of Volvo Group" as "Bad English."

I find that brilliant.

"Bad English" means that, in a conversation, each person should speak a level of English that the other person can understand. If, say, an American fluent in English is speaking to a Korean who is not, and the Korean doesn't understand the American, then it is the American who is not speaking correctly. Bad English means that it is okay for a person who is not very good in English to speak up anyway. The less fluent English speakers in an organization are encouraged to speak up. The native speakers are encouraged to aim at being understood, instead of flaunting their most advanced English. The focus moves to the message, and away from the grammar. Remember: It is not necessarily the person with the biggest vocabulary who has the best ideas.

According to a study I read, just four percent of all English conversations are between two people both fluent in the language. Ninety-six percent are conversations where at least one person does not have English as his or her native tongue. That means, I guess, that "Bad English" is the official language of the world…

By the way, this whole book is written in "Bad English." Being a Swede, English is not my native language, but I have chosen to write this book in English anyway. I did so as a celebration of the idea behind "Bad English"—that we should encourage people to dare to speak—and write—their own English in order to get their thoughts and ideas out to the world.

TAKE AWAY

If you—like me—are not a native English speaker, be inspired by Volvo Group and begin to communicate your ideas in your best English, however bad it might be. What you have to say is more important than how you say it.

If you are a native English speaker, encourage non-English speakers to speak up. By inviting everyone to speak, you are helping create a broader dialogue, which will increase the chance of information and ideas getting spread around the organization.

Can You Have a Google Passport?
Recruiting without borders.

SCENE: THE GOOGLEPLEX

More precisely: The outdoor café at the corporate headquarters complex of Google at 1,600 Amphitheatre Parkway in Mountain View, California. I was having a smoothie with Rikard Steiber, Global Marketing Director for Mobile Ads at Google.

BACKGROUND

My first question to Rikard was, "Is Google a global company or an American company?" He pondered this, then said, "We are on our way to becoming a global company."

In many ways Google already is. The company has more than a billion (1,000,000,000!) users in 200 countries and territories, which means one in seven people on the face of the Earth is using a Google product. Not bad for a company founded 14 years ago.

I asked Rikard to explain how Google had been effective in building a global company. Rikard looked around at the people sitting at the small tables and explained, "One of the most interesting things with the Google headquarters is that we have people of so many different nationalities, religions and cultures working side by side. Google's recruitment process is very good at finding people with the same values, regardless of what country they might come from."

As Global Marketing Director for Mobile Ads, Rikard's working day is a microcosm of Google and the world. He has a small team of 25 people reporting to him—literally spread out around the world—in London, Paris, Hamburg, New York, San Francisco, Tokyo... and, of course, Mountain View, California. Rikard uses email, phone, video chat and other electronic tools to communicate with his team members, who work together with teams in the local markets to develop new and innovative advertising solutions for the mobile market.

After discussing how global the work environment at Google is, Rikard corrected his initial comment. As he once again looked around at the people sitting under the colorful parasols at the tables in the café, he said, "Actually, what makes Google interesting is not that we have a lot of nationalities working here—but that we have *no* nationalities working here! They are all just "googlers.'"

TAKE AWAY

The better a company's recruitment process is at making sure that the people who come into the company have the same values and beliefs, the stronger the corporate culture becomes. The stronger the corporate culture becomes, the less relevant nationalities become. And the less relevant nationalities and borders become, the easier it will be for people to cross them in order to work together with the people who happen to be the best people to work with for any specific task... no matter where they sit. Are you doing that?

Share Your Mind...
How Mindshare shares ideas across the world.

SCENE: THE SHANGRI-LA HOTEL IN KOTA KINABALU, BORNEO

It was at their 2011 Asian regional conference at the Shangri-La Resort hotel in Kota Kinabalu, Borneo, that I was first introduced to Mindshare. I was there to give a keynote speech, and during the conference I spoke to some of the Mindshare employees about my upcoming book on global companies. It quickly became clear to me that Mindshare was one company I just had to include in my book. A few months later I was in London to learn more about this interesting company. The more I learned, the more impressed I became.

BACKGROUND

Mindshare calls itself "The Global Media Network," and that is not just a slogan. With over 113 offices, this media agency has more than 6,000 employees in over 82 countries. They have no global headquarters, a flat structure, and 80% of their business comes from global clients. That's not bad, considering that the company, which is a member of the WPP Group, was created less than 15 years ago.

"When we launched the company, people thought we were mad. When they heard what we named it, they laughed," Nick Emery said to me. As Global CEO of Mindshare, Nick has been with the company from the start. Back then, the concept of a global media agency working across borders with global clients was frowned upon. With the assumption that media and advertising, like many other businesses, should be local, few saw any advantages in creating a media agency with global reach.

But Nick and his colleagues did not launch Mindshare for what the world used to be like: They launched it for what the world would become.

"We were set up for this world. We built [the company] for the modern world," Nick explained, adding, "And we picked our name for a reason."

The reason? "Sharing." The most important skill in an interconnected, rapidly developing world.

Nick looked at me and said, "It's about sharing across borders, across competencies, across clients. It's about spotting trends and seeing ideas." Then he added, "The answer is not [only] in London or New York anymore…"

What he said reminded me of a passage on the Mindshare website. Under the heading "Who We Are," the company writes:

"[…] because the future arrives faster in some industries, countries, even cities, we can rapidly tailor what we learn in one sector or region to another. Which means our clients benefit from the very latest knowledge, expertise and insights they would probably otherwise be unaware of."

To ensure I understood the importance Mindshare places on the sharing of information, Nick said, "If you see something, you can quickly change." He left it to me to conclude that if you do not see something, you cannot adapt to it. Many companies may have operations around the globe, but they do not have global operations. And global sharing of information does not happen by itself.

As one Mindshare employee put it, "Without [actively developing and nurturing] the network, 'global' is just a nice word."

I asked Nick how they were able to maintain an ethos of sharing. As with so many fundamental truths, the lesson is easy, but the mastering hard. "It's not difficult—but it is hard work." Then he began to tell me about some of the things they do.

For starters, all salaries, bonuses and KPIs (Key Performance Indicators) are set centrally. Everyone at Mindshare works for the same company, and compensations are therefore aligned around the globe. The company has two global conferences per year and global calls between all the leaders every other week. Their IT systems are aligned across the company, and so on.

But most important is the focus on sharing at Mindshare. It is not just about processes—it is about a mindset. A client win for Mindshare is celebrated throughout the organization, whether from Peru, Vietnam or New York.

When the Mindshare office in Moscow had some problems due to low morale, the company offered some of the employees at that office the chance to transfer temporarily to India and New Zealand to get new inspiration, new ideas and new energy, by seeing how things work in other parts of the world. The intention was that they could then take these ideas back to their Moscow office and implement them in their own market. It was not meant as a perk, but as a way to get the office focused on being part of the sharing of information across the network again.

One of my favorite stories about how this culture of sharing manifests itself at Mindshare is a story about an email sent in error…

A while back, someone intended to send an email to a small group of Mindshare employees, but mistakenly chose an email address that sent an email to every single Mindshare employee. All 6,000+ of them! Quickly, people from around the world started making funny replies to the obviously misaddressed email—and they did that by pressing Reply All, flooding everyone's mailboxes. The IT Department considered shutting down the entire email system because of the pressure those thousands of emails put on the IT infrastructure. But the CEO wouldn't let them.

"This is exactly what Mindshare is about!" he exclaimed. And no, Mindshare is not about overloading the IT system with jokes. But it is about building a culture of sharing.

How many companies with more than 6,000 employees in 113 offices do you know of that have an email system where anyone, anywhere, can email everyone else in the organization—including the CEO—with a single email?

Of course, this "email-all" address is mostly used to share great work and communicate important announcements. But occasionally it is used for other purposes, such as sharing a joke.

I asked a woman at the London office of Mindshare what this meant to her.

"We get this email from Bolivia saying 'We are entering this competition,' and then someone in Russia wants us to reply to a survey, and then suddenly there is an email from a woman in Poland who wants to tell [all of] us about this cookbook that she has written. [Reading these emails] you get a feeling of 'Wow, we really work for a global company…' It makes us proud."

I asked what this commitment to sharing created. Nick thought for a moment before answering, "It allows us to be more free, more flexible, less limited—and faster. It is also more democratic. And it creates a structure to enjoy change. It is in our DNA to be a global company."

An organization is defined as "a social group which distributes tasks for a collective goal." The word "organization" is derived from the Greek word "ergon" (as in "organ"). It means "a compartment for a particular job." Maybe what Mindshare has figured out is that the best organizations are not actual organizations, meaning they do not see themselves merely as "compartments," and they do not just "distribute tasks." They encourage and thrive on the sharing of information. Sharing, to quote Nick Emery again, "across borders, across competencies and across clients."

How often do you do that? As a company and as a person?

TAKE AWAY

How many of the people in your mobile phone address book are in a different country from you? How many are from another culture? How many emails do you receive or send across a border? How many of the web pages that you visit on the World Wide Web are from around the world? Enough? Honestly?

Notes

"One Company. One World. One Source." OPW, A DOVER COMPANY

SKF: A Global Case Study
How a 100 year old international company became global.

SCENE: CHINA WORLD HOTEL IN BEIJING

I had my choice of Chinese Peking Duck, Japanese sushi, Indian Tandoori Chicken, or a sea of shrimp nestled under a swan carved out of ice. There were 600 of us from all over Asia attending the SKF ASIA Pacific Distributors Convention. At the opening dinner reception, we mingled in the ballroom of the China World Hotel in Beijing—aptly named, it seemed, for the occasion. The buffet featured a wide variety of international offerings.

Going with the theme of a global evening, the organizers provided an interesting twist to the band playing traditional Chinese songs: The singer was not Chinese, but a blond Caucasian women from Europe, singing in what seemed to be flawless Chinese. SKF had obviously invested a lot to make this a successful event. After all, Asia is a very important market for this world-leading bearings company.

During dinner I had the opportunity to have a long discussion with SKF Global CEO, Tom Johnstone. I was curious how a bearings company founded in 1907, which had well-established operations in Europe, Asia, Africa, North America, and Latin America as early as the 1920s, looked at the concept of *"One World. One Company."*

BACKGROUND

Tom Johnstone began by telling me the history of the company, "I remember seeing an interview where someone was talking about the importance of having a presence in the BRIC markets. Well, we were selling in China in 1912. Russia in 1916. India in 1923 and Brazil in 1914. By 1932, we were in 40 countries."

He was obviously quite proud of how quickly his company built a successful international business. So I asked him, "How was SKF able to become such an international company so fast?"

He began telling the story about how there were many domestic bearing companies already present in each of the main European markets. The only way for the new Swedish startup challenger to compete was to go where the competition was not, which meant going out in the world. "We did not have a home market," explained the CEO.

According to the SKF CEO, SKF is not a "Swedish company." "We have a Swedish heritage, but we are not Swedish." When I asked him "So, if you are not Swedish, then what are you?" He answered with a big smile on his face, "We are SKF!"

He continued, "We are a global company, with Swedish values." He then clarified, "We have these common values—a base—but we are a Swedish company...in Sweden, and SKF is a Chinese company in China, an Indian company in India, and a German company in Germany."

To stress how important this mindset was to him, he added, "The best compliment I have received was when I was in the U.S. and met with an Indian investor who said, 'I was born in Bangalore, and I grow up next to an SKF factory. All the time growing up I thought that SKF was an Indian company. All the people working there were Indians.'"

The best compliment the CEO has ever received was when an Indian investor thought SKF was Indian? This is a CEO who gets excited when people do not know the origin of his company. SKF is global, and that's exactly the way he likes it.

When did SKF go from being "international," meaning being a

"Swedish company with operations internationally," to being a "truly global company?" I thought he would answer, "1940" or so. I was wrong by almost half a century…

Tom explained how he had been traveling to Asia on business for the last 25 years, and how Asia continued to grow in importance. But, less than 10 years ago, something happened: Growth really took off, and China went from being an "emerging market" to one of the most important markets for SKF. The world had changed, and therefore so had SKF.

Johnstone pinpointed the time when SKF had to start behaving as a global company to the shift of importance of the markets in Asia, especially China. "I would say [it happened] in 2005, when we brought 150 of the top managers to Shanghai for our annual conference. I still remember sitting in a taxi on the way into Shanghai from the airport, with a Swedish manager who had never been to China. He kept staring out of the window, mouth open, saying "Wow." That [conference] was a defining moment for the company." With the rapid, almost explosive growth of China and the rest of Asia, it was impossible to continue to be a "Swedish company." Or as Tom put it, "We stopped 'selling to Asia' and started to 'develop in Asia.'"

And grow in Asia they do. SKF is opening two new factories in Asia each year, and hires 1,500 new employees every year. With more factories, employees and customers in Asia, SKF became global. Today, SKF has 100 manufacturing sites and 15,000 distributor locations in over 130 countries.

With 3,500 employees in its native Sweden and more than 5,000 employees in China, the concept of SKF as a "Swedish company" becomes absurd.

Additionally, SKF has started to move its R&D to Asia, and will soon have 400 people in their Asian R&D centers. SKF used to have its motorcycle products' R&D in Italy (since Italy was a major player in two-wheelers in the 20th century). However, with the explosion of motorcycles sales in India in recent years, it became clear that the new global epicenter for two-wheelers would be India. So SKF moved its R&D center from Italy to India. "You need to develop close to the customers," explained Johnstone, "and the customers moved." So SKF moved as well.

After the move to India, the rate of innovation from the R&D center exploded. Johnstone is convinced that this increase in innovation would not have happened if they'd kept the center in Italy. Moving an R&D center from Europe to Asia is probably easier for a company that has been international for over 100 years and which already had R&D in more than one place. Johnstone thought it might be more difficult to make these necessary moves for a company with all its R&D and other corporate functions in one place. But he insists that companies still need to move important functions closer to the markets.

He ended our conversation with a bit of advice to his fellow CEOs, "You have to let go," he said. "We need to change into a [global company]—not be changed by [globalization]."

TAKE AWAY

A global company has no exports, because it has no "home market" or "export markets." Instead, it has "markets" and "clients." When this way of thinking becomes second nature, you realize you cannot "export" to someone close to you. So, the closer you are to your customers, the more absurd the idea of exports becomes. How close are you to your customers?

Notes

Notes

"One World One Company" CARGO LOGISTICS

The World Runs SAP

SAP goes to the world.

SCENE: THE SAP OFFICE IN SINGAPORE

The reception area at the SAP office in Singapore is larger than many companies' entire offices. I was recently there to ask a series of questions about innovation to Simon Dale, Head of Technology and Innovation at SAP Asia/Pacific/Japan. We sat down in two big chairs. Behind us was a massive wall of television screens playing an animation about SAP.

One of the animations read, "SAP: Turns questions to innovations." So, let's start this chapter with a question about SAP and innovation: Where do you think SAP has its research center?

BACKGROUND

Well, if you guessed its research center is at its headquarters in Walldorf, Germany, you would be correct.

But you'd also be right if you answered Montreal, Palo Alto, Vancouver, Belfast, Darmstadt, Karlsruhe, Zurich, Bangalore, Pretoria, Ra'anana, Brisbane, Singapore, Sydney, or Tokyo.

I asked Simon Dale why SAP has 20 research locations in 12 countries. He began by saying, "We are still expanding!" It seemed as though he thought I was suggesting that 20 different research centers was too few! As it turns out, SAP has a very open minded and broad view on innovation.

Basically SAP finds where the world's most interesting academic research is being done, and then opens up a research center targeted on the same theme next to this university, making sure that SAP gets deep, and direct, connections with the world's best experts on this field.

One example of this is how SAP, in cooperation with EDB, recently opened a research center in Singapore focused on urbanization and logistics. SAP is hiring 100 people, of which at least 25 are PhDs, to research new ways to use software to improve the way we build cities and transport things. Of all the places on Earth, they decided to put this research team in a small city state on the equator. This makes perfect sense, since Singapore is one of the most urbanized countries in the world, with the world's best airport and the world's busiest shipping port. By sitting next to these experts, the SAP researchers get close access to the latest research, which they can then channel to the rest of the company—and to SAP customers around the world.

Another example of how SAP puts its research centers near the talent was when SAP decided that China would be the place for their research on the cutting edge work of in-memory computing. Why China? "We built a great team of around 45 Chinese PhDs there. They are the best in the world. We give them free rein to experiment on the new technology, to find new business applications that were not possible before—even dreamed of," explained Simon Dale.

I was very intrigued by SAP's approach to research. Instead of trying to lure the most creative people in the world to their headquarters, SAP turned the question on its head and asked, "Where is the most interesting academic research being done?" Then they put one of their research centers there.

I asked Simon Dale if there were added advantages to the strategy of having so many different research centers dotted around the world rather than just the close connection to world leading experts. He answered, "You won't get real breakthrough innovation if you limit your thinking. You have to have people who think differently. And if you want different thinking, you cannot rely on a single mental model [the Western way of thinking]. If we have Chinese researchers, they think differently from an Indian researcher or an American researcher." He sat back in his big chair and repeated his message to stress his point, "I do not think we should limit ourselves."

Clearly SAP is not limiting itself, and it's apparent the strategy is working. When we were nearing the end of our interview, I asked Simon Dale to describe SAP to me. His reply was simple, "We are the world's largest business software company." And the company is doing great. The share price is currently at its highest since the dotcom craze of 2000, and SAP just reported its best year in its 40-year history.

The company has over 180,000 customers worldwide. Its 55,000 employees are unusually widely spread out around the world. Of its 15,000 developers, approximately 6,000 are in Germany, but more than 2,000 developers are in China, 4,000 in India, and hundreds in Vietnam, Korea, the U.S., other European countries, and so on. SAP is not focusing so much on where they come from, but on what they are doing… and why. With this approach, they can deliver the best solutions in the world by tapping into the best research in the world.

TAKE AWAY

Where is the world's most leading academic research being done on the subjects that are most relevant to your company's future? Do you have your research center next to them? If not, why not?

Notes

"One World One Company, to manage all your Logistic needs." TNL LOGISTICS

It's Not a Small World — It's a MINI World

How one car brand moved into a global position.

SCENE: THE MINI OFFICE IN GERMANY

It was Friday afternoon in the MINI office in Germany where Jörg Dohmen was sitting in his office. It had just become Saturday morning in Singapore, and I'd just come home from an evening out with friends. Before Jörg could call it a day, and before I could call it a night, we needed to make one more phone call. We picked up our phones to have a conversation about brand history and globalization from a MINI perspective.

BACKGROUND

Jörg Dohmen is Brand Strategy Manager for MINI, the small, and very successful, car favored by modern metropolitan city dwellers around the world. This cute little car has 4.3 million fans on its various Facebook pages, and 285,000 of those cute little cars were sold in 2011.

I started our conversation by asking him a question, "To many people, most car companies are very much connected to a country—Japanese cars, American cars, German cars, and so on. How do you approach that at MINI?"

He replied, "We are not limited to one country. We are proud to be an international brand, certainly with British roots."

Jörg explained that, when they re-launched the MINI in 2001, being perceived as a British car was not a good thing. "At that time there was a saying that went, 'You need two British cars in order to have one running.'"

So MINI wanted to distance itself from the perception of being British. But, of course, it did not do that by trying to become a "German brand." MINI is owned by BMW—and some might therefore argue, more or less angrily, that "the Germans stole the MINI brand from the British." But Jörg doesn't give much credence to arguments like that. "The thinking of 'one car = one country' is an old story, and an old discussion," he said.

MINI moved on. Because the world did.

"It is a new business battleground." Jörg said and he then went on to explain how the car industry is becoming increasingly more global. There are people of over 70 nationalities at their plant in Oxford. The MINI is sold in over 100 countries. The MINI Countryman is made in Graz, Austria; the diesel engine, developed by the BMW Groups R&D center in Munich, is made by PSA in France; a wide variety of products in the car are made by international parts suppliers like Bosh, Magna, and so forth. Parts in a MINI can be traced to production facilities in a long list of countries—and a lot of the design is done at the BMW Group's office in Germany.

Jörg himself is an example of the new "internationalism" of the car industry. He was born in Germany, studied in France, Barcelona and Toronto, sits in Germany, and has a British boss. Fittingly, he oversees the global brand strategy of the MINI.

"MINI is inviting, warm hearted and unconventional. It is all of that. But it is not a one-country brand," he explained.

Jörg provided me with examples of how they managed the transition from British to global while remaining proud of their heritage.

They took the iconic MINI with the Union Jack flag on its roof, and launched MINIs sporting flags of 26 other countries. During the FIFA World Cup in Germany, they lent out MINIs for one night to people from around the world so that they could drive around waving their home country flags in celebration of their own country's national team, communicating, not a specific country, but the brand values of the MINI—"inviting," "warm hearted" and "welcoming." Making the MINI global did not weaken the brand, according to Jörg Dohmen, "Disconnecting ourselves from a specific country made us more independent. It has strengthened the brand."

I ended our phone call by asking the Brand Strategy Manager of MINI what the next step is for a global brand like his. He laughed and shouted, "Let's go to Mars!" It was obviously a joke, but it was a joke from someone who doesn't let national borders define what is, or is not, possible.

My biggest take away from the conversation I had with Jörg Dohmen was how he looked at branding from the point of where you are more than where you came from. He said, "When you define your brand identity, you need to identify what it stands for [right now] and then execute on those strengths. Yes, we are proud of our British heritage, but a brand has to be not so much about where you come from, but what you are—and where you are going."

TAKE AWAY

In a sense a brand is like a person. You need to remember where you came from, but it is more important to remember who you are—and to remember where you are going.

Where are you from? Where are you now? Where are you going?

Notes

"One World, One Company, One OS." Microsoft

"Heimskur"
Do not be a moron.

SCENE: REYKJAVIK, ICELAND

Iceland is exotic. I knew that before first setting foot there in 2008. A land of active volcanoes and hot spring baths where you can swim outside in the midst of winter—and the land of singer Björk.

However, when I was invited to Reykjavik for a series of business talks by Aðalsteinn Leifsson, the director of MBA programs at the University of Reykjavik, I still did not fully understand how exotic my trip would be. Mr. Leifsson would take me swimming in sub-zero arctic seawater, where we literally had to push the icebergs away to be able to dive in. He would take me sauna bathing in a tepee on the Icelandic tundra, and he organized a guided tour for me to visit the places where the "hidden people" live. Not, from my experience, the normal itinerary set up by a professor of a business school when you come as a guest speaker.

Then again, Iceland is not your normal place. It is part average northern European country, part fairy tale.

BACKGRUND

It was fitting I found out about the word "Heimskur" during one of my trips to Iceland. It is a word that dates back to the mystical times of the Vikings, and continues to be applicable for the world today.

"Heimskur" is an old Icelandic word dating back more than a thousand years. The Icelandic Vikings used "Heimskur" to describe the people who never ventured outside of their farms in Iceland. It means "moron."

As a Viking, you were supposed to build a ship, recruit a crew and sail away to other lands. The purpose of these trips was to get new ideas, insights and impulses on anything from how to make weapons to how to farm. And, true, part of the purpose was to steal as much gold, silver and swords as they could. As the Vikings saw it, a person who did not open up to the world to find new ideas from other cultures was a moron.

I guess the Vikings could be called the entrepreneurs of their time—bold, adventurous risk takers traveling into the unknown to find new ideas.

Too many people limit their potential, their creativity, and—in the end, their lives—because they are not embracing the human spectrum of creativity in its entirety. They are not taking full advantage of the potential of the world, because they are not living in the world. They are stuck in their own corner looking inward, viewing what is different as "foreign," and looking at anything that is foreign as "strange."

TAKE AWAY

You are not a Heimskur, are you? Venture out in the world and find more ways of doing things. In the end, if you come to the conclusion that the way you are doing things is best, then so be it. But how can you be sure that your way is best, unless you first find out what other ways there are to do what you are trying to accomplish?

Focusing on Ports vs Focusing on Passports

How the global financial crisis pushed Maersk, the world's largest shipping company, toward becoming more global.

SCENE: THE MAERSK OFFICE IN SINGAPORE

As one of the world's largest shipping companies, Maersk Line operates more than 600 vessels capable of shipping a total of 3,800,000 20-foot containers at any given time. That may sound like huge amounts, but somehow it fails to explain the vastness of the company. Consider this:

If you were to place all the Maersk Line containers one after the other, they would reach from Denmark to Australia, via Cape Town. If those containers were stacked on top of each other, they would stand approximately 2,500 kilometers high. For perspective, consider that the International Space Station is orbiting at 400 kilometers from Earth. On just one of its largest ships, the Emma Maersk, they can ship 746 million bananas in a single trip.

I sat down with Peter Baker, Director of Human Resources for Asia Pacific Region at Maersk, and started our conversation by asking him how the global financial crises affected them. His reply was straightforward,

"We lost a boatload of money."

He then explained how Maersk was able to use the momentum of the crises to implement long-overdue changes to become more global.

BACKGROUND

Shipping has been global for hundreds of years. In the early 1400s, the Chinese Admiral Zheng He sailed all over Asia, reaching India and even the Horn of Africa. Columbus sailed to the "New World" in 1492, and Magellan's expedition of 1519–1522 was the first to sail around the world. Yet shipping companies have often been very much connected to a specific country. Maersk is no exception. The company has 25,000 employees across 325 offices in 125 countries, but the company is still very Danish. Maersk was founded by a Dane in 1912. Their current CEO, Søren Skou, is a Dane, as were all previous CEOs before him. Additionally, all country heads in Asia (except in New Zealand and Taiwan) are Danes. Until recently, so were all the second level managers as well.

But the global financial crises propelled Maersk toward becoming a more global company. "We obviously need to change," Peter Baker said to me. I asked him why this was obvious.

As it turned out, the first reason was financial. For the longest time Maersk kept all corporate functions in Denmark and, as I mentioned, almost all managers and country heads around the world were Danes—and Danes are expensive. When the company started to lose money in the crises, they scrambled to cut costs. First, the company began moving back-office function and customer support from Copenhagen to Manila and Mumbai. "We are a global company, so there are cost savings in moving work to locations with lower labor costs," explained Baker. But there were other advantages as well.

Baker clarified, "[Having almost only Danes] is not sustainable. Our [non-Dane] employees need to feel that, one day, if they are good enough, they are going to get that job. When people start to feel that skills—not passports—are what get you promoted, it generates a very positive momentum [in the organization]."

According to Peter Baker, this shift was also driven by their customers, who had become more global in the past few years. He mentioned Thailand as an example. "Our biggest clients in Thailand are the 'Japanese' car companies, who use us to ship auto parts from Thailand to markets in Asia, the Middle East and Africa." He added, "So it's good to have local leadership that reflects the diversity of our customer base."

Recently Maersk also started to move more important corporate functions outside Denmark, including the global center for stowage from Copenhagen. Stowage, in layman's terms, means "where to put the boxes on the ship"—a crucial competency since wrongly stowed containers can cause a ship to sink. For one hundred years this important function was based at Maersk headquarters in Denmark. Then the company realized it made more sense to have it in Asia since a vast majority of the world's cargo is loaded onto ships there. It is now based in Singapore—the busiest port in the world.

Maersk is on a journey... but they are not there yet.

Even though most of the Maersk ships, from a legal standpoint, sail under Singaporean flag, it still helps to be Danish on board. Crew are generally employed under the terms and conditions of their home country, meaning that a Danish captain earns a much larger salary and has more generous provisions for time off than a Filipino captain.

But what if all captains, regardless of passport, got the message that their salary would be based purely on performance? If all of them felt that if they saved fuel, they had a chance of doubling their pay? Would that not incentivize the Filipino captains to work harder? Turns out that this is an issue that Maersk is still struggling to resolve.

With 25,000 employees across 325 offices in 125 countries, it does not make sense for a large portion of them to feel that in order to reach the top, they need to have a Danish passport.

So Maersk has a way to go. Nevertheless, the company is starting to change, and the change became apparent in 2008/2009. Within ten years, Peter Baker hopes that most country heads will be local. It took one hundred years to make the shift to being a truly global company, but now they are pushing for the change to happen.

"The local talent can be as good as the Danish," Baker acknowledged. "We just needed to find the right people and train them well." He added, "Local talent is also far less costly than expatriates."

Baker ended our interview by emphasizing that lowering costs is not the main reason Maersk is doing this. The main reason is customer focus. "Our customers are becoming more global as well, and they are demanding a consistent product regardless of where they ship the box from and regardless of where the box is going. We are not doing this because it is 'nice' to be global. We are doing it to better serve our customers. They will not choose us because we are bigger—but because we are better. So we need the best people out there."

Maersk takes pride in being the most reliable shipping company in the world. For many years, Maersk built its history around being founded by "a Danish captain from a small Danish shipping village." It was meant to communicate the spirit of Danish captains who went out to sea with a mentality of doing nothing wrong. But by changing the narrative from a "Danish captain with a make-no-mistake mentality" to simply a "captain with a make-no-mistake mentality," the focus shifts onto the skills of the captain instead of his passport. Suddenly any Maersk seafarer, regardless of origin, can be inspired by the history of the company... and feel that he, or she, is part of it.

TAKE AWAY

A passport is not a skill—or at least it shouldn't be. Maersk is working hard to become as global in its organization as it is in its operations. How about you?

Notes

"One world, one company, all of your needs." BUEHLER

Build It (Great) and They Will Come

A refreshing look at how Evernote is not run as a company.

SCENE: THE EVERNOTE HQ

When Phil Libin founded Evernote, he told investors he planned to have ten million users in three years. Some people laughed at the bold statement. I am guessing those same people are not laughing anymore. Evernote was launched in open beta mode on June 24, 2008, and went from zero users to one million users in 15 months. On June 6, 2011, three weeks before their three-year anniversary, they passed the ten-million-user mark. I booked an interview with Libin to find out more about the rapid success of his company. The first thing I learned was that he is not running a company—he is running a service.

BACKGROUND

The main product for the company, Evernote, is called... Evernote. It is an extremely flexible software that makes it easy and hassle free to save and collect things you want to remember—everything from screenshots, recipes and receipts to photos and ideas.

I began my conversation with Libin by asking him to describe Evernote.

He said, "It is an external brain for everyone [designed] to make you smarter."

I have met many CEOs that love to talk about their company. Phil loves to talk about the product.

I asked a more specific question, "So what is the company Evernote?"

He seemed genuinely confused by the question, and said, "They are really the same thing. The company Evernote exists to build the service Evernote. It is one thing."

After having interviewed hundreds of senior managers over the years, I find this uncompromising focus on the service instead of the company very refreshing. The Evernote team has an invigorating way of looking at many things, like their business model.

Evernote software is free to download, and you can use it as long as you want without ever paying. Of course, there is a premium version that costs money—but a vast majority of users are using the free version. That's the way Evernote planned it. Offering a free version makes it risk free to try it out. Users of the free version rave about the product to their friends, providing free user-generated marketing.

Evernote also had a refreshing approach to the way they launched.

"We did not do market surveys or a plan for which markets we should focus on," Phil explained. They never thought about launching in their own "home market" first—instead they built a product for the world…from the start. They were able to get their product into many different markets and languages from the beginning by launching translate.evernote.com, a site where users can translate the program to the language of their choice. That means that one of 30 or so language editions that Evernote is available in is Urdu, another one is Telugu, and so on.

On translate.evernote.com the company states: "Our objective is to make Evernote available to the entire world. With your help, we can achieve this goal. We have deployed an easy-to-use online tool that allows you to translate as much, or as little, of Evernote as you like. There is no minimum commitment. Translate one line of text or an entire client—it's up to you."

According to Libin, building the product for the world from the start added perhaps ten percent in developing costs. It was a gamble that paid off. Today, just one third of Evernote's users are in the United States. Building for the world let Evernote increase their user base by 300 percent.

Evernote never saw itself as "an American company." When asked why some companies still insist on looking at themselves as coming from "a country,'" Phil got quiet for the first time during our interview, until he replied, "That's a good question…"

Evernote is not focused on "markets," not on "paying customers," and not on "the company."

They are simply focused on building a great service.

Phil explained why they use this strategy by saying, "Something changed." I asked him to elaborate.

"All the founders of Evernote had been running companies before. We used to be like many other companies, who spend 30 percent of their time and resources on developing the product—and then 70 percent on other things, like sales and marketing to get people to buy it. Then something changed."

The thing that changed was us, the customers. We learned to use the Internet to find out what other people actually thought about a product. We learned that the Internet could be used to tell the world about what we liked and did not like.

We may have gained access to the Internet fifteen years ago, but it took a while for us to change our behavior. But now we have. That means companies need to change their behavior as well. Which is exactly what Evernote did, focusing all their attention on building a great product, and not so much on marketing or selling it.

"If you build something that you love, there is a big chance there are millions of others who also will love what you build. And people love to talk about the things they love," Libin said.

Then he gave a bit of advice that sounded so obvious that it took a while to realize how refreshingly unusual it was.

"If you build a great product, people are going to find it."

I asked him to give me an example of how this thinking has been successful. "Let me tell you about Japan," he answered, and started doing just that.

Even before they had a Japanese version, Evernote saw that they had a lot of users in Japan early on. Libin made a point of stressing the value of measuring everything, from growth to number of users, so they could pick up on when things started to take off.

When they saw the increase of Japanese users they flew to Japan to "see why it was getting so popular." They met with users, had dinners with bloggers, studied and listened. What they discovered was that Evernote was perfect for the Japanese culture of collecting. Japanese blogs and Internet forums were exploding with enthusiastic users raving about the service.

Libin ended by adding, "So then we invested more in Japan..." he stopped mid-sentence and corrected himself. "...we invested more in the product to suit the Japanese users." It might look like semantics, but it is crucial to how Phil views Evernote. They did not "invest in Japan"—they "invested more in the product to suit the Japanese users."

And it paid off. Twenty percent of the ten million users are Japanese, and since the Japanese have a higher tendency to pay for the product, close to thirty percent of revenue is coming from Japan.

More importantly, all the excitement in Japan around the product also meant they received inquires from big companies in Japan, like Sony and other electronics companies, to bundle Evernote with their products — and those bundling deals were made worldwide.

The old way of running a company would be: *Start with your own home market and then do research on where you should go next.*

The new way of running a company is: *Think global from the start and act on where you get the best traction from your users.*

I guess you could summarize it by saying, "Talk and ask less. Listen more."

Before we ended our discussion, Libin expanded on his thought about building a great product for the world, "If you build a great product, people are going to find it." Then he added, "and if they do not find it, then per definition it's not a great product…"

Read that second part one more time: *"And if they do not find it, then per definition it's not a great product…"*

Something changed. You used to be able to control when you launched a product in different markets. You used to be able to control who found out about your product, who talked about it, and what was said. You used to be able to control the conversation — which meant you could control the situation.

Then something changed. And the best way to react to this change is to focus on what you can control — which is building a great product and making sure that the people who find out about it can get it, regardless of where they are.

TAKE AWAY

Theodore Roosevelt is often credited with saying, "Build it and they will come," supposedly referring to the Panama Canal. Regardless if it was he who said it or not, he was right. The Panama Canal was a hit. Phil Libin and his crew at Evernote have added one word which makes all the difference. "Build it GREAT and they will come." I am fairly confident that is what Theodore Roosevelt meant.

Now the question for you, of course, is: Are you putting all your efforts on building the best possible product in the world using the entire world as your inspiration? If not, why on earth not?

HQ – Don't Let It Go to Your Head(quarters)

What we are calling our main corporate office
— and what it signals.

SCENE: SINGAPORE

I was sitting by the pool of my condo in the heart of Singapore trying to find an interesting example of a company that is practicing the idea of a "heartquarters," when I remembered John DeHart—a fitting surname for this story, by the way.

John DeHart is the cofounder of Nurse Next Door, an innovative care giving company that has grown quickly in Canada and the U.S. over the past ten years. On his blog, DeHart shares some of his ideas about why the company has been so successful. The company has been rated as the #1 Place to Work in British Columbia, in addition to being named as one of the top places to work in Canada, and one of the top 20 most innovative companies in B.C.

Under the headline "Lesson #16. A Culture Has its Own Language." John writes:

"At Nurse Next Door, we also have our own language. Some people think it's weird, and that's OK. The people who think it's weird simply don't fit our culture. (One reason this works in building culture is that it is another "self select" mechanism, where those who don't "fit" will really stand out.)

"It reinforces our own core purpose, and core values, at every interaction with our company. When Nurse Next Door franchise partners need to call the head office, they are not calling "corporate," they are calling Heart Quarters."

BACKGROUND

The idea that a company somehow has one single place where all the important thinking is gathered—like a body has a brain that does all the thinking—is really a weird metaphor. Weird and wrong.

Maybe companies like to use the term "HQ" because it's a military term. Some like to compare business to war, using terms like "kill the competition," "battle for market share," "invade new markets."

Compare that to the definition of a corporate version of a HQ: According to Wikipedia, a corporation's headquarters "denotes *the location where most, if not all, of the important functions of an organization are coordinated.*" (My italics.) The idea of a place where "most, if not all, of the important functions of an organization are coordinated" is dangerous for any company wanting to become a Truly Global Company (a "TGC").

Likening the corporate office to a head may make people working at that office think that they are more important than is healthy for a company.

If you are working in the main corporate office of your company, thinking that you are the "heart of the organization" is, I think, a better—and more sympathetic—attitude.

How about "Heartquarters?"

The head does the thinking, but the heart does the feeling. "The place that makes sure that our corporate values are strong, solid and shared" should be the main purpose of a HQ. A heartquarters does not tell others exactly what to do; its main job is to keep its finger on the pulse of the organization. By sending out oxygen, it gives energy and resources so that the rest can do what they need to do.

Just to be clear, I am not saying that you should change the name of your HQ from headquarters to heartquarters, since made-up words risk sounding corny. (But, frankly, isn't "headquarters" as corny as "heartquarters," just more familiar?)

What I *am* saying is that I hope that your organization thinks about how using the wrong corny metaphor can lead to too much centralization, making the company too slow, too stale and too rigid in a dynamic, rapidly changing business environment.

TAKE AWAY

Ask yourself, if you are—or were—working outside HQ, would you like to get impulses from the head telling you what to do, or impulses from the heart giving you energy to do it? And if you are—or were—the CXO in a company, would you like to be part of the brain—or part of the heart?

Notes

"One World. One Company. One Goal." XYLEM INC.

Going from A Towards B

Global: A journey that never reaches the destination.

SCENE: THE ECONOMIST

In 1843, a very global-minded hat manufacturer named James Wilson founded "The Economist" newspaper "to further the cause of free trade." Wilson was very much a global person himself. Born in Scotland, he ended up being buried in Kolkata, India. Statues of him can be seen in both the UK and Hong Kong. Way back in 1938, half (!) of the 10,000 copies of his newspaper were sold internationally.

Today, the newspaper is run by The Economist Group—a company that calls itself "a global media company that develops intelligent brands for the intellectually curious." And global this newspaper truly is. Currently, The Economist has more than 1.5 million subscribers worldwide. Only 200,000 of them are in the UK.

Just like its founder, The Economist has evolved from something British to something global.

It was in this spirit of free trade, globalization and "curious intelligence," that I sat down with Tim Pinnegar, Managing Director Asia Pacific for The Economist, to talk about how The Economist Group is living up to the grand global vision of its founder.

BACKGROUND

It took The Economist 161 years to get to one million subscribers. It took them seven years to go from one million to one and a half million—and that seven years was during a period when most newspapers sales declined. Clearly there has been an increased interest in a newspaper that writes intelligently about the world.

Tim Pinnegar explained, "We have always written about the world. The difference is that the world is now interested in the world. We basically have the same content as we have always had. But [before] there were not as many people who wanted to read about it. Most people didn't have to know anything about [say] India or China 10 to 15 years ago. [Today] the world is doing business with each other."

Pinnegar told me that The Economist has "benefited hugely" from the increased interest in the world. One example of this is how the terrorist attacks of 9/11 made Americans much more interested in what happens outside their country. As a result, The Economist went from 350,000 subscribers in the Americas in 2000, to 850,000 today.

The Economist may have been about free global trade all along, but the company was for many years run more or less from the UK. Ten years ago, they had no African office, no office in the Middle East, and no offices in India or China (not counting Hong Kong).

But in the last few years, a lot of things have changed. Today, The Economist has editorial offices in Atlanta, Beijing, Brussels, Cairo, Chicago, Hong Kong, Johannesburg, Los Angeles, Mexico City, Moscow, New Delhi, New York, Paris, San Francisco, Sao Paulo, Singapore, Tokyo, and Washington D.C. — and more offices are on the way.

"Gone are the days when you could run [The Economist] out of the UK," said Pinnegar.

I asked him what the advantage was for running a global news organization from around the world. He answered, "It gives us flexibility, speed and empowerment." The company is now closer to their customers and can react faster, and the people who work in the different offices feel that they can make things happen.

According to Pinnegar, The Economist is for "global, intelligent, curious people" who want a newspaper that "takes you to interesting places you didn't know you wanted to go." He told me, "We believe that a reader in Mumbai has more in common with a reader in Massachusetts than with his neighbor."

As a global media brand with similarly minded readers, the company has done many things in the last few years to become more truly global. Virtually all the content in the different editions of the newspaper is the same around the world. For their most important clients, they now have Global Key Accounts. Sales people in the organization now get commissions for more than just selling in "their" region, regardless of what product they sell and to whom.

It is not uncommon in the company today to see scenarios where a sales person based in Singapore sells a sponsorship to a China-based company for a conference on Africa taking place in London.

The company also has global management meetings where leaders from around the world meet to discuss the future of the company. The last one was in Rome.

But even good things can be improved. The increased global focus for The Economist has yet to reach the top management. If you are part of the management team or on the board of The Economist, there is a 13 percent chance that your name is John, and there is a zero percent chance that you are from South America, Africa or Asia.

One could discuss if having a diverse leadership team with people from different cultures around the world is a necessity for a company with such global ambitions as The Economist. Would having a more diverse management team be simply cosmetic? Or would it be symbolic? Or is it, in fact, essential in order to be able to really report on the world?

Pinnegar describes the process of becoming a global company as a journey of going "from A to B"—a journey that companies can embark on. It is clear where he wants The Economist to be. As he puts it, "B is a much better place to be."

Few, if any, organizations have fully reached "B" and become "truly global" companies, but The Economist is rapidly becoming more and more global as an organization, after making huge changes in the last few years.

TAKE AWAY

Hidden in the lower left corner of the contents page of every copy of The Economist is a short paragraph that reads: *"First published in September 1843 to take part in 'a severe contest between intelligence, which presses forward, and an unworthy, timid ignorance obstructing our progress.'"*

What a wonderful sentence. Here is a newspaper founded to take part in a severe contest between intelligence and timid ignorance. How brilliant and grand.

Ask yourself: How is your own organization battling ignorance?

Be inspired by the bold vision of the founder of The Economist. Take note—and take advantage—of what is happening in the whole world. Press forward with intelligence, instead of obstructing progress with ignorance.

Standing on the Top of the World
About the global divide.

SCENE: THE OFFICE OF OGILVY & MATHER

David Mayo is a busy man. In addition to being head of Ogilvy in ASEAN, he is, at the time of this writing, also temporarily CEO of Ogilvy Philippines, as well as CEO of Ogilvy Indonesia. That means that he spends two days per week in Manila, two days per week in Jakarta, and one day per week in Singapore—when he is not traveling. Despite his hectic travel schedule, he was able to squeeze in 30 minutes to talk with me about how Ogilvy views being a global organization.

It turned into such an interesting conversation that Mayo cancelled his scheduled meetings so we could keep talking for another hour or so.

BACKGROUND

After I told Mayo the theme of my book, he began by saying, "Heritage is very important. But geographical heritage is perhaps not so important." Ogilvy was founded by a Scottish man who moved to New York in 1948. But that is not the core of the Ogilvy & Mather culture.

"Our culture is not built around a country, but around a person," David added. But not just any person. The founder, David Ogilvy, was a remarkable man. He arrived in New York with no connections, no clients, and no network—but with a passion and determination to create great advertising. Today, the company that bears his name has more than 450 offices in 169 cities around the world. With more global clients than any other advertising agency, the client list at Ogilvy & Mather includes companies such as Coca-Cola, IBM, and Duracell.

David Mayo is a good example of someone who acquired a global mindset. When he was 24 years old, he was offered a choice: Accept a new job as the company he worked for merged with another company, or accept one year's salary on the spot. He took the money—and for the next 18 months traveled the world.

Upon his return to England, he realized he had two passions in life—travel and advertising. So in 1993 he moved from his native England to Hong Kong.

I asked him how he was affected by having a global mindset. Like all good storytellers, Mayo likes to talk in metaphors. "The world shrunk, and thereby I widened my horizon," he said, then continued with an analogy I found quite interesting.

"When you have a global mindset, you look at the world the same way a person on top of a mountain looks out over a valley. You get a wider perspective, a better overview, a holistic understanding. A person who never travels is like a person standing at the bottom of the mountain looking up. To him, the rest of the world looks unapproachable and out of reach. The world becomes difficult."

When asked what the biggest advantage of standing on top of the mountain was, as compared to being stuck in the valley, he replied, "You see more. And you realize that not everything is black or white—that there is a huge range of shades of gray, and it is in these different nuances that the fun is found. I look at many of the people I left behind in the UK, and I genuinely feel, 'They could have a much richer life.'"

TAKE AWAY

When our interview concluded, Mayo stood up and shook my hand, offering these final words, "When an organization gets a global mindset, you get closer to putting the full potential of the organization to better use in the world."

It sounded so obvious when he said it, yet so few companies are really committed to it.

Are you utilizing the full potential of your organization? Are you standing on top of the mountain looking out? What do you see?

Notes

"One World. One Company. One Message." ARDYSS LIVE UK

Stardoll

Reach for the stars. Reach for the world.

SCENE: THE STARDOLL OFFICE

I had never seen an office quite like the one where I met Mattias Miksche. The first thing to catch my eye was a huge rococo mirror with a golden frame. Big pink flowers were painted on pink walls. The furniture in the waiting area could best be described as "cute." It looked more like a dollhouse than the office of a successful company—which, of course, was the whole point, since the company I was visiting was Stardoll, home to Stardoll.com, a site where children from around the world can play dress-up with virtual dolls. I sat down to talk with Mattias Miksche, CEO of Stardoll, about how thinking globally equaled success for his company.

BACKGROUND

The history of Stardoll is unusual. Its predecessor was founded in 2002 as Paperdollheaven.com by a 58-year-old Finnish cleaning lady. She launched the site on a shoestring budget, doing all the site illustrations herself. Slowly but surely, more and more kids from around the world found out about the site. It started to grow.

After a few years, she recruited investors and a management team, and the growth took off. Today, the site boasts more than 110 million children and teenagers as registered users from over 200 countries and territories worldwide. At the headquarters, now located in Stockholm, more than 130 employees from 35 different countries run the show for the over 20 million users visiting the site each month.

"We felt from the start that we had a global hit," explained

Miksche. "But because of our background, we grew differently from most other sites." In the early days of the company, the founder focused more on building the site she wanted to build, instead of thinking much about where in the world the kids were going to use it. It turned out that, thanks to the borderless properties of the Internet, kids from all over the world found out about this cool site where they could play with dolls.

When the new management came in to increase business, they were, in Miksche's words, "not big in one country, but pretty big in very many countries."

That was a good thing.

"We had no boundaries from the start, and I think that affected the way we run the company," Miksche said. Other websites for kids, like Habbo Hotel, had tailored their sites after countries, but Stardoll chose to build just one site that was more or less the same no matter where you logged in from. The only difference, which is slight, is that female dolls in the West wear panties and a bra before you dress them, while female dolls in Saudi Arabia wear a small slip dress.

"Saudi Arabia?" I remarked. "You have users in Saudi Arabia?"

"We are huge in Saudi Arabia!" He replied with a laugh.

While planning for world domination, the new management created a list of countries they wanted to venture into, taking into consideration the size of the country, Internet penetration, the willingness of people to pay for content, and so on. The finalized list did not include Saudi Arabia—nor did it include Turkey or Poland, yet those three countries are currently some of Stardoll's biggest markets.

"We did have a patronizing view of some of the countries that are now our biggest market. Luckily, we were able to snap out of that. We have been positively confused about some of the countries where we grow the most. And I think we have now grown to understand that a twelve-year-old girl in one part of the world is more or less like twelve-year-old girls everywhere else. She dreams about being a rock star, a model, or a princess."

The success of Stardoll in these so-called unexpected places gave the company an advantage over all the copycat virtual doll companies that began to emerge. There were times when it seemed that a new virtual doll company was starting every day. However, the vast majority of them were from the United States and focused solely on growth in the U.S. While the competition was focusing on America, Stardoll was focusing on the world.

Not all companies do.

Stardoll is approaching other companies that target the children's market to put together sponsorship and promotional campaigns with them, but they frequently meet with companies that only want to do deals on a per-country basis.

"I am surprised every day by how un-global a lot of so-called global brands are," observed Miksche. With a more global outlook, these companies would get a much better return on their investment—for less work—than what they currently get.

TAKE AWAY

The argument can be made that it is easier for Internet companies to behave as global companies due to the borderless nature of the Internet. However, that risks sounding more like an excuse than an explanation.

Instead of looking at Stardoll as an "Internet company for kids," it might be more useful to think of them as a "company for kids, that is using the Internet."

Many other companies targeting children could have gone from zero to 110 million users in a decade. But not all kids' companies have the insight for borderless thinking that Stardoll does.

What opportunities would open up if you adopted borderless thinking as well?

All Business is Local?

How Jones Lang LaSalle and the real estate business went through real changes in the last few years.

SCENE: THE JONES LANG LASALLE OFFICE AT HANOVER SQUARE, LONDON

The history of the London-based real estate company Jones Lang Wootton could be traced back to 1783. In 1999 the company merged with American public company LaSalle Partners to become Jones Lang LaSalle—one of the largest truly global real estate companies in the world. Today they have 40,000 employees doing business in 1,000 locations in 70 countries.

My meeting in London with Charles Doyle took place in his office in historic Hanover Square, which seemed particularly appropriate. Developed as an exclusive residential address in the early 18th century, Hanover Square is now a premium office location. Doyle is Global Chief Marketing Officer and Head of Research for Jones Lang LaSalle and is based in London, even though the global headquarters is in Chicago. We met in these historic real estate quarters to talk about how the commercial real estate business has suddenly changed into a global business.

BACKGROUND

The strapline for Jones Lang LaSalle (JLL) is "Real value in a changing world." So how has the real estate market been changing recently?

Passionately, Doyle started telling the story, "Well, let's look at this company. We have been local since the 18th century, international since 1950, and truly global for the past five years."

According to Doyle, many industries became global thanks to

technology (like the Internet companies), or thanks to supply chain development (like some car companies). "In our industry, the borderless flow of capital into property, and the expansion of multinational corporations across the world, is what made [the commercial real estate industry] global. It started in the 1980s, but went into super drive after 2,000. It's becoming a global supermarket for commercial property. Now you get cities like Dubai where the majority of the buyers and tenants are foreigners."

In cities like Singapore, twenty percent of the buyers of condos do not even live in the country. And in London, the prime locations are not just for the British anymore. They are being purchased with capital flowing in from around the world. Doyle looked out of his window at the properties his company was currently selling on a global market, and said, "This is a glimpse of the future."

He proceeded to tell me how his company had just bought King Sturge—a London-based real estate company which for over 250 years (!) had thrived by selling local property in London and the provincial UK cities. By 2011 they realized that, in order to remain strong in the local London market, they needed to be able to compete with global real estate companies with access to global clients and capital flows. So they agreed to become part of the Jones Lang LaSalle family.

"Not everyone will like it, but commercial real estate companies who cannot globalize—or specialize in a niche market—have a difficult future ahead. There is no such thing as a purely local market anymore. Everything is influenced by global forces."

That last statement might be stretching it a bit, but he definitely had a point. A few weeks before my interview with Doyle, Jones Lang LaSalle had announced yet another global deal. In a press release, aptly signed off from "London, Singapore, Chicago,"

Jones Lang LaSalle explained how they would now be the single global real estate provider for GlaxoSmithKline's 80 million square feet of real estate across 750 locations. Jones Lang LaSalle was chosen based on "its expertise, capabilities, pricing, and global scope." In the press statement, Sue Pictor, Director, Global Real Estate, GlaxoSmithKline said, "We are excited to partner with Jones Lang LaSalle to evolve our global real estate strategy." JLL has similar global deals with Volvo Cars Corporation, UBS, HSBC and Doosan Power Systems, among others.

"In a world where the buyers are more and more global, we have to be global, too," Doyle explained. "Our clients are taking us with them around the world. When they open an office in India, their Indian staff need a building to sit in. We can find, purchase or lease, and manage that building for them. Regional or national players cannot compete at this level of global contracts. They have to focus on the smaller local clients, as they don't have the balance sheet strength and international connections with buyers and sellers that we do." He added, "Local [real estate] companies are an endangered species unless they are very specialized in a niche area. The big corporate and investor deals are being taken care of on a global level."

I asked him to list some of the advantages of becoming a global player.

"Scale, reach, strong balance sheet, and a powerful and unified brand make a big difference. We can get international deals that the smaller companies can't bid on. Technology is another. With a global business we can develop more advanced solutions and roll them out across the company. We can also invest more in knowledge and research, obviously. Our market knowledge at every level is unparalleled. And then there is the access to the global capital. [As a global company] you add a new dimension of value at scale, market power, recognition and connections globally, nationally and locally."

TAKE AWAY

Some could debate that "all business is local." And, arguably, real estate is the most local business there is, as you cannot easily move a house or a plot of land. The last few years have shown that what used to be true is not true anymore.

The saying has to be upgraded from "All business is local" to "All business is local—except the business that is global."

What business are you in? The local or the global one? Which one would you prefer?

A Nobel Man

And a traveling man.

SCENE: KUALA LUMPUR, MALAYSIA

In May 2011, the Swedish Embassy organized a "Swedish Dinner'" on the theme of "Nobel." Hundreds of guests were invited to a gala dinner in the spirit of the Nobel Prize. A chef was flown in from Sweden, accompanied by the ingredients he needed, for a Nobel Prize Dinner at a 5-star hotel in Kuala Lumpur. The organizers were even able to get former Malaysian Prime Minister, Mahathir Mohamad, to be one of the two keynote speakers. I was the other, and was flown in from Singapore to speak on "Swedish creativity."

The emcee of the event was Mr. Alfred Nobel himself. Or, to be exact, it was actor and Nobel expert Peter Sund, a man who makes a living impersonating Alfred Nobel. Mr. Sund had also been flown in from Sweden for this event to talk about "Sweden and creativity."

It is understandable that the Swedish government wants to promote Sweden using Alfred Nobel. However, as I would find out by chatting with Sund during the event, it is not entirely clear that Alfred Nobel would think using himself as an example of "Swedish creativity" was such a great idea.

BACKGROUND

Yes, Alfred Nobel was a Swedish citizen, and yes, he was born in Sweden in 1833.

But if we had a chance to sit down with Mr. Nobel in "inventor heaven," he would not describe himself first and foremost as a "Swedish inventor and businessman." Rather, he would consider himself to be a "traveling inventor and businessman," because what made Alfred Nobel a great creative businessman was not that he was Swedish, but that he traveled.

When he was four years old, his parents left Sweden and moved the family to Finland. They later moved to St. Petersburg, Russia, where Alfred Nobel went to school. The young Alfred traveled to many countries including Germany, the United States, and France. He was fluent in five languages (Swedish, Russian, English, French and German), had laboratories in five countries, and started companies all over Europe and in America.

Alfred Nobel invented dynamite, the invention that made him famous and rich, while living in Krümmel, Germany. So, technically, dynamite is not a Swedish invention, but a German one.

When Alfred Nobel died, the lawyers had quite a job figuring out which country he "belonged" to. He had a magnificent apartment in Paris, a big villa in San Remo, Italy (where he died), and a house in Sweden. In the end, the courts decided that Karlskoga, Sweden, should be regarded as his primary home, but only because of an old rule that said that the primary home should be decided by "wherever the person had the most number of horses." Had that decision not been made, it is unlikely there would be any Nobel prizes, since his relatives questioned the validity of the will. The rest is history.

For over 100 years, the Nobel Prize has been the most prestigious prize in science, literature and peace. In his will, Nobel stated that the prizes should go to those who "during the preceding year, shall have conferred the greatest benefit on mankind." And for the peace prize, he specifically indicated it should go to a person who has "done the most or the best work for fraternity between nations, for the abolition or reduction of standing armies and for the holding and promotion of peace congresses."

The medal for the Peace Prize is inscribed with the text "Pro pace et fraternitate gentium" which translates to "For the peace and brotherhood of men."

TAKE AWAY

Alfred Nobel was a creative genius, a brilliant businessman and a great visionary. If we want to be inspired by him, we should acknowledge that, more than anything, Alfred Nobel was a man of the world—a curious, constantly traveling businessman. Or, as author and thinker Victor Hugo called him, "Europe's richest vagabond." That is how we should remember him; not as "a Swede," but as a traveler of the world. Now, can that inspiration translate into making you more of a traveler of the world?

Notes

"One World One Company." DEWSOFT

Global Power: Manpower

Recruiting without borders.

SCENE: JÖNKÖPING, SWEDEN

A few hundred of the highest managers of Manpower in Sweden gathered in Jönköping, a midsize Swedish city with a huge convention center. At the beginning of the conference, they showed pictures from the previous night's party. The theme was "Berlin," and obscure photos of Swedish recruitment managers dressed up as hookers, transvestites and S&M-fetish-gays flashed by. It was a surreal experience that made it obvious that the management of Manpower Sweden had created a relaxed and fun working atmosphere.

I was in Jönköping to talk about the value of doing things differently, so my only regret was not flying in the night before so I could have participated in the party.

After my speech, I had the chance to sit down with Peter Lundahl, CEO of Manpower Sweden.

BACKGROUND

Manpower is a world leader in the employment services industry with operations in 82 countries. Their objective is to make it easier for companies to fill their job openings.

Lundahl explained the recent transition in the market. "There has been a dramatic change the last two years," he said. The change he is referring to is the way the customers of Manpower are now recruiting. "Our job is to recruit the best people to our customers regardless of country. That might even mean that we go to one of our competitors in another country, if that is what it takes to find the right person."

Lundahl talked about how Manpower was offering "borderless candidate solutions"—solutions that clients didn't ask about as recently as a few years ago.

At that time, Lundahl said, Manpower was looking for forklift operators anywhere they could find them, for a client in Denmark, Rumania, anywhere.

My reaction to what he described was that it sounded like a lot more work. He sighed and laughed at the same time, and said, "Oh yes! It is so much more work!" When I asked him why they continued to do it, he explained that his clients were now asking for it. They were demanding that Manpower find the manpower, regardless of where they were. And if that was what the clients were asking for, that was what they had to do. Yes, it was more work for Manpower, but a better solution for the client. And in order to be able to deliver a global solution to their clients, Manpower was forced to become more global itself.

TAKE AWAY

How big is the pool of persons from which you are choosing? How big could it be?

AMEX — Earth Express?
When nationalistic thinking limits business opportunities — and business thinking.

SCENE: SCHIPHOL AIRPORT TRANSFER TERMINAL

While in transit on a KLM flight from Singapore to Stockholm, I walked by an American Express booth at Schiphol International Airport in Amsterdam. A friendly sales person approached me and asked, "Would you like to sign up for an American Express card and get KLM frequent flyer miles on every purchase?"

I actually did. Since I often flew on KLM, and since I bought a lot of tickets and hotel nights using credit cards, that actually made total sense.

So I said, "Yes, please."

BACKGROUND

The sales person asked for my Dutch address and Dutch banking details, and prepared to sign me up as a customer.

When I explained that I was living in Singapore, he stopped and explained to me that since I lived in Singapore, I had to sign up for the card in Singapore — and that I could only get credit for miles on Singapore Airlines.

"But I want to become a customer now," I said. "And I want to get KLM miles — not Singapore Airlines miles — since the KLM flights from Singapore to Sweden are the best flights for me."

But he could not sign me up. And I am sure the sales rep was following procedure. As a test, I have also answered, "Yes, please," when being approached by American Express staff at airports in Helsinki and Stockholm — with offers to get bonus miles on Finnair and SAS. Every time, I have been turned down when they realize I am living in the "wrong" country. They obviously do not want me as a client.

There are two fundamental flaws in the way American Express approaches their potential customers at these international airports.

1) They assume that a person living in one country wants to get points *only* from the carrier based in the same country.

2) They have installed a process where, in each country, salespersons are only allowed to sign up customers living in the same country.

In a perfect world, the person at Schiphol Airport in Amsterdam would have signed me up as a customer from Singapore who could receive points to be used on KLM.

If legal or regulatory issues restricts them from signing up customers from other countries, American Express could instruct their sales staff to get the potential client's phone and email contacts to be forwarded to the potential client's "home" country.

On its website American Express labels itself as a "global services company," and in many ways they are. Its 58,300 employees around the world make sure their customers can spend more than 600 billion US dollars per year using their 88 million American Express cards. Nevertheless, that number could increase if they were truly thinking and acting as a global organization.

It is unlikely American Express is losing huge amounts of revenue because they demand that only people living in one country can get bonus miles from a carrier based in the same country. However, after speaking with the sales staff at Helsinki Airport, it is also clear the company is turning down a lot of business. A frustrated young salesperson told me, "I would love to sign up all the customers who come here asking to become customers, but I am not allowed." When I asked if it was common that non-Finnish people try to sign up, he replied, "Yes, I turn down a lot."

The company's inflexible policy of signing up customers only from the customer's own country shows that even a company that has had international operations for over 150 years, which operates in 130 countries, and which calls itself a "global service company," still can let the boundaries of borders limit their ability to offer what the customer wants.

TAKE AWAY

What business opportunities does your company miss because of business processes built around borders instead of customers?

It might be a symbolic example more than anything else. But what does American Express's procedure say about the way they run their business? Is this way of thinking making the company miss other business opportunities? Would a company called "Earth Express" make the same mistake?

Notes

"One World, One Company." CMEDIA

Bankers Hiding in Their Castles and Chalets?

When HQ gets disconnected from the rest of the company.

SCENE: HONG KONG

The day started with a Chinese breakfast in Singapore and ended with a seafood dinner in landlocked Beijing. It was one of those days where the concept of a small world became clearer than ever to me. That same day I also met with the HR manager of a Scottish bank for an Italian lunch in Hong Kong. During the interview it became painfully clear that some companies have not been able to make the necessary transition to global performance.

BACKGROUND

The person I had lunch with will remain anonymous, but he works for RBS (Royal Bank of Scotland). A passionate and ambitious HR manager for RBS, based in Hong Kong, he grew up in another former British colony. As he described his current employer's attempts at being global, he became more and more frustrated.

"Nothing happens in the UK," he complained. "They like to sit in their Scottish castles and think they are in control, but they have no idea—no understanding—of what is happening over here."

The idea that the company headquarters always knows best, but at the same time doesn't put enough effort into understanding what is happening in the offices around the world, is something he referred to as "corporate colonialism," an eerily apt description of the strategy some companies adopt in an attempt to go global.

When asked what he, as an HR professional, thought the management of a company seeking to succeed globally should do, he answered, "It's about letting go. HQ needs to stop deciding what is the good thing to do—and instead learn where the best things are being done. You need a genuine understanding of what is happening. Good things can happen anywhere." He ended his frustrated rant about the company by adding, "It's about breaking down the silos—and HQ is the biggest silo there is."

As he was talking about the managers sitting in their Scottish castles hiding from the rest of the world, I was reminded of an interview I did with another frustrated banker in Singapore who worked for a "large Swiss bank." He told me, "We have managers who are just sitting in their Swiss chalets." He, too, was frustrated by the way his bank had centralized risk analyses in Switzerland instead of placing it close to the changing markets. When asked what this centralized thinking leads to, he replied, "We lose the advantage of being close to the market. And that means increased risk and missed opportunities."

TAKE AWAY

How much freedom is your company giving to people in the organization to think for themselves and come up with the best solutions? How good is your organization at identifying optimal practices around the organization and making sure those practices are spread as quickly and effectively as possible to other parts of the company?

Peer-to-Peer Management
How Ericsson changed the way they learn.

SCENE: ERICSSON HEADQUARTERS
IN STOCKHOLM

Petter Andersson is Vice President for Learning & Development at Ericsson. I met with him at the Ericsson headquarters in Stockholm to talk about the way Ericsson has become more of a global company during the last decades—and how Learning & Development is changing as a result.

Ericsson has always been an international company. Founded in Sweden in 1876, it was in South Africa in 1896, Russia and Australia in 1897, and Mexico in 1905. But, for the longest time, it was also a very Swedish company. Just ten years ago, Ericsson had about 100,000 employees worldwide, but nearly 50,000 of those employees were in Sweden—a country that has less than 1% of the world's information and communication technologies (ICT) market. Today, Ericsson has more than 100,000 employees, but less than 20% of them are in Sweden. Ericsson became more global.

BACKGROUND

I asked Petter why this shift of workforce happened. "It's mainly a combination of services growth and an increase of R&D activities in different parts of the world. A general ongoing globalization is, of course, a reason, but it's also the result of our customers wanting us to perform services locally to a higher degree. To be successful in today's ICT market, any player needs to create value by building on scale efficiency and through local utilization of global competence. The ICT market is under tremendous change, and we continuously need more and more people where our customers are."

I asked him what the biggest difference was between an Ericsson with 80% of the staff outside Sweden and an Ericsson where 50% were Swedes.

"Actually, I don't think the proportion of staff itself tells a lot," he replied, "but rather how the shift happened. During the IT/Telecom crisis in 2001, Ericsson, like many others, had tough times. The workforce was reduced by half. It was painful for everyone, and especially for the people who had to leave. For those of us who remained in the company, I got a sense that the crisis brought everyone together a bit more than before. That sense of belonging and mutual dependencies naturally shapes a global culture.

"Over the years, I have also seen an increasing awareness among most employees of the role ICT plays in the world, and how we affect people and society. Being a company with a truly global role in society is great for people to feel. It impacts the whole working spirit to have a clear purpose."

Petter added, "A consequence of shifting the workforce mix is, of course, to continuously improve the balance between global standards, local decisions, and customers' proximity."

So I asked Petter how to maintain and evolve this balance as well as the culture.

"First, people need to know the purpose of an organization. This is the common denominator for everyone to be engaged around. Second, people need to share the same values in their work. Third, in order to understand the different viewpoints, it's important for leaders and others to move around and learn from each other. This is not achieved by business trips flying in and out for a day, but by creating the mobility and understanding of perceptions from a deeper perspective."

Represented globally for decades, the introduction of new ICT technology made it possible for Ericsson to take it to a new level. Systems and tools are helping processes and professional networks to become global.

Petter explained how new digital tools have made it easy and affordable to share knowledge quickly across the organization.

What, then, becomes the role of the Learning & Development function in Stockholm? It is to help provide the tools so that people in the organization can create their own material and share it easily with others, thus creating a culture of learning.

It all makes sense.

Ericsson is a world leader in information and communications technology, and is now using these tools itself to connect the employees around the world by empowering the person with the information to communicate it directly to whoever should have it. Let's call it peer-to-peer management.

Let's end this chapter with the same sentence that started it: Petter Andersson is Vice President for Learning & Development at Ericsson. Or, to be precise, he was when I interviewed him! Petter began our meeting by informing me he was moving on to another position as Head of Learning Services based in Beijing for awhile. When he told me why he was leaving a vice president job at corporate headquarters, I was inspired.

"I could feel my own alarm bells going off. Being at the same place for six years started to affect me. I understood that I wanted, and probably needed, to look for new perspectives and to challenge myself again, not to become complacent." So Petter chose to leave the headquarters and move to the other side of the world to work with customers in order to gain new insight, new inputs and new inspirations.

How about that, a Vice President of Learning & Development who leads by example by walking the talk!

TAKE AWAY

The word "inspiration" literally means to "breathe in." Inspiration is oxygen for our minds. It gives us energy to create new things —both as individuals and as organizations.

We all know what happens if you live in a small confined space for too long, breathing the same air over and over again. You die.

Are you getting enough inspiration? Is your organization breathing well? Are you?

To Turn an Aircraft Carrier Around

How a crisis made Siemens change for the better.

SCENE: THE LOBBY OF THE MARINA BAY SANDS HOTEL

Huge. The word is fitting to describe the interview I had with Nicolas von Rosty of Siemens. We met in the huge lobby of the Marina Bay Sands Hotel to talk about the huge transformation that this huge corporation had undergone in the last few years. While we are at it, let's define "huge." Siemens has more than 360,000 employees.

Siemens used to be a very very German company. Or, as Nicolas von Rosty, Corporate Vice President of Siemens AG said to me, "We were too German, we were too white, and we were too male." Who would have thought that a huge scandal could propel Siemens to change this? That is exactly what happened, and it is a fascinating story.

BACKGROUND

In 2008, Siemens was sentenced to pay fines and lawyer costs of more than 2.5 billion Euros in penalties for having paid more than 1.3 billion Euros in "suspicious payments" between 2001 and 2007.

It was, as I mentioned, a huge scandal, but as the saying goes, "A crisis is a terrible thing to waste." Siemens used that crisis to shake up the company.

There was a turnover of 90% of the board, 70% of the second layer of management, and 50% of the third layer of management.

This in a company with more than 70 billion Euros in revenue and operations in 190 countries. They hired a new CEO. For the first time in Siemens' history, he was recruited from outside, and he was not from Germany.

The new CEO, Peter Löscher, was born in Austria, studied in Hong Kong and the United States, married a Spanish woman, had worked all around the world, and spoke German, English, French, Spanish, and Japanese. Suddenly, Siemens had a global CEO instead of a German one.

Since they were replacing so many top positions, the company made a conscious effort to recruit a more diverse management team. The country head in China was no longer German, but Chinese. In most countries with a Siemens presence, German Country Heads were replaced by "locals," and this happened over a very short period of time.

"Normally, you cannot do [a change like that] so quickly," said Nicolas von Rosty, "but we had just fired almost all our leaders so we could do it."

You do not shake off 160 years of too much "German-ness" just like that, but Siemens has transformed itself.

"Siemens of today is not the same Siemens as five years ago," explained von Rosty. "There is now not a single leader who doesn't have a global mindset."

I asked him why it was so important to have a global mindset.

"Initially, you have to connect with your peers [of colleagues around the world]. If you don't understand them—you cannot leverage the knowledge of Siemens. But it is also important to be closer to the customers." He concluded, "Finally it is important in order to lead diverse teams."

In the "previous" Siemens, it was an advantage to be a white German male, because you knew how to get along with the other white German males. Now it's important to have global exposure so you can get along with the others who have global exposure.

Of course, there is nothing bad with being German; the point is that it is now not an advantage either. Previously, white German male leaders would hire other white German male leaders—not because they were better, but because they were similar. Familiar.

Too many times, someone would recruit a specific person because they "liked the guy," or because it was someone they knew. Today, Siemens has a worldwide recruitment system focusing on the person's skills. They have an integrated database with knowledge of the skill sets of all 360,000+ employees. Three years ago, they did not have that. "We are now looking at the competence, not the person. And today we know more about what we know about our employees," said von Rosty.

Today the company will not promote anyone to a top management role who has not worked outside their native country for at least a few years. They also put extra effort into making sure that people from developing countries get a chance to work in other places. In many companies, leaders from developing and emerging markets do not get a chance to have global exposure, because the perception is that they are needed to take care of the rapid growth in the developing markets they come from. In turn, this lack of global exposure stops them from receiving senior positions. To make sure that talent from the developing world has a chance to advance to the top, Siemens runs a special two-year program where top talent from developing markets get the opportunity to work in the developed world.

I ended my interview by asking von Rosty what the difference is between a manager with global mindset and one with the old Siemens mindset—apart from the fact they are better at handling diverse teams and have a better understanding of the world. He replied, "You broaden your horizon."

I asked him to explain.

"To broaden your horizon means that you can grasp new business opportunities. You think outside the box—and you see the whole box—not just your corner of it. You listen before you act, you take others' opinions seriously, you are open to new ideas, and you are not afraid to leave your comfort zone." In short, you end up with more creative managers.

A diverse organization is like a open mind. The more viewpoints and ideas you are exposed to, the more synapses you create. The added synapses, in turn, create more ideas. Siemens realized that, and went all out to create a more diverse and globally minded organization.

At one point, von Rosty likened Siemens to an aircraft carrier. It had the global reach of a huge aircraft carrier and the resources, power and strength to go anywhere and compete with anyone. The CEOs for the local Siemens companies are the fighter pilots —fast, flexible and responsive. Without them, an aircraft carrier is just a very big boat that turns slowly. By having diverse teams that understand the local markets and know how to talk to people from other backgrounds, Siemens ensures that this massive company competes successfully around the world. He calls it "One Siemens."

TAKE AWAY

If a company of 360,000 employees can refocus to perform more as one, what is stopping you?

Mergers vs Acquisitions
AkzoNobel and the mindset of "us."

SCENE: A BALLROOM IN HANGZHOU

More than 100 top leaders of AkzoNobel Surface Chemistry (a business unit of AkzoNobel) recently gathered in the Chinese city of Hangzhou for a global conference. The conference ended with the screening of an animation about AkzoNobel's commitment to diversity. In more than 1,500 conferences for hundreds of companies in over 40 countries, I have never heard a bolder—and more honest—statement of an organization's determination to become a global company, while at the same time highlighting what still remains to be done. After hearing it, I knew I had to learn more about this company.

When the conference was over, I sat down with Dr. Dale S. Steichen to talk about how AkzoNobel is transforming itself into a much more global company—and why that is a great thing.

Dr. Steichen was the right person to interview. Dr. Steichen, an American, holds the position of Global Vice President for Research, Development & Innovation at AkzoNobel Surface Chemistry—and he has been with the company for 21 years. He has seen the transformation of the company towards becoming more global.

BACKGROUND

AkzoNobel is a merger of the Dutch company Akzo and the Swedish company Nobel, as well as a series of other chemical companies. For many years, these different companies continued to behave as separate entities instead of being "One" AkzoNobel. "There was very much a 'we and they culture' before," said Dr.

Steichen. That led to mismanagement of resources, a lot of internal politics and back-stabbing, and a lack of cooperation. "People had wounds in their backs [from being constantly stabbed in the back]," remembered Dr. Steichen, looking genuinely disgusted. He told me about how things used to work — for example, how one American kept writing condescending and rude emails to colleagues in Europe, just because they were from Europe. I asked him how they dealt with things like that and he replied, "You have to have managers who squash things like this like a bug!"

The mentality of looking down at others and trying to optimize your own division instead of thinking of the best for the whole company led to a silo mentality within the company. That affected innovation negatively. As Dr. Steichen put it, "An idea that just sits in a silo gets nowhere." Things needed to change.

So in the 1990s AkzoNobel embarked on the ambitious journey of transforming into a truly global company, and in 2002–2004 this ambition intensified.

"Our clients pushed us," said Dr. Steichen. "Our customers are global, more so than us! We are lagging behind the Unilevers and P&Gs of the world." Then he added with a smile, "But we are more global than the other chemistry companies…"

AkzoNobel's global customers want a supplier of chemicals able to deliver the same high quality product regardless of location — and they want someone who can do it consistently. As a result, AkzoNobel set out to build factories that were more or less identical all over the world, whether in Sweden, China, the U.S. or Brazil.

"You can copy/paste one of our factories onto another," explained Dr. Steichen. "The products are the same. The processes are the same. And, most importantly, we have the same safety standards, the same environmental requirements, the same way of working, and so on."

That is an interesting statement. While many people still talk about the difference between developing countries and developed countries, AkzoNobel decided to have the same —high— quality and standards regardless of the factory location. "We do not look at our South American factory and say, 'That's a South American factory.' It's an AkzoNobel factory."

This fresh way of working together as one company is also apparent in how the company works with developing new products.

"We are not bidding against each other [for new projects] any more," said Dr. Steichen.

"There is no 'my project'—it's all 'our projects.' No one [any longer] gets all worked up about where we put a project, or thinks that the 'interesting projects' have to go to Holland [where the headquarters is]. People now realize that we will—and shall—put projects where it makes most sense to put them—and base those decisions on facts, not historical or geographical biases."

I noted that he seemed happy with how it worked now. He replied instantly, "Oh, this is sooo much better. It's been an amazing transformation!"

Dr. Steichen credits the fact that his company is a merger of different companies as one of the reasons that AkzoNobel is now more global. Mergers alone will not make you global but it can help weaken the negative effect of having a too-powerful headquarters—if it is done the right way.

Dr. Steichen stated, "Whenever you incorporate a new company, it has to be a merger of equals—regardless of the size of the two companies. You cannot look at two managers and say, 'This person is smarter because he comes from the bigger company.' You have to take the best one."

As I listened to him, I realized he was saying that a company should never make an acquisition; they should only make mergers. Legally, it might of course be an acquisition, but practically it always has to be a merger between equals. An acquisition means "an act of purchase of one company by another" (We buy you), while a merger means "a combination of two things into one" (We combine us).

By evaluating whatever is good in the new company — be it processes, values, ideas or whatever — and being able to incorporate that into the original company, the company becomes stronger and better every time… instead of just bigger.

Listening to Dr. Steichen, I could tell that AkzoNobel was really trying to live by that. But he also warned not to take it too far. "It's not about everyone being the same — it's about everyone pulling in the same direction."

TAKE AWAY

Dr. Steichen ended our interview with a graphical metaphor, "It's like if you have a horse, a donkey and an elephant. You don't want them to lose their different strengths and personalities — but you *do* want all of them to pull in the same direction — as one. If you can achieve that, you can achieve magic."

Borders are Boring
When behavior changes, do you?

SCENE: SOMEWHERE AT A COMPUTER

The Internet has been in our lives for over 15 years, but it takes a while for us to start changing our behavior. Many times it feels as if companies are changing their behavior slower than customers are. Vast majorities of people are still buying most of their things locally, but increasingly more and more people want to buy things where it is most convenient or cheap, even if it means crossing a (mental) border online. Once you start doing that, it is very easy to get used to. While it seems many companies are doing what they can to stop people from becoming customers, the customers are finding creative ways to get what they want anyway.

BACKGROUND

Some examples:

Hulu.com will not offer TV shows to people outside the United States, so a consumer learns to download software that tricks the servers to think he's watching from the U.S.

Many sites in the U.S. will only ship to an address in the U.S., so people in Singapore, for example, get a Vpost account that gives them a fake U.S. address (and phone number), so the goods can be shipped to that address, only to be re-shipped automatically to Singapore. (Vpost is a service run by the Singapore Post Office.)

Apple or Amazon won't allow you to download a song because you are in the wrong country? No problem. Buy yourself a gift card and use the gift card to send yourself a gift.

A German who wants to buy locally goes to eBay Germany, and doesn't realize that many items offered for sale at eBay Germany are actually posted by Chinese. When the order is placed, the products are shipped from China using DHL.

Does your mobile phone operator insist on charging ridiculous fees when you travel across a border or call another country? You download Skype, Viber, WhatsApp or Rebtel, and use a service not so confined by borders.

A Filipina living in Singapore, trying to get ahold of the American TV series West Wing, found it would be cheaper to order from eBay in Australia than to buy it in Singapore. So she placed the order. But when the box arrived, it was in an box from Amazon Germany. In the box was a note: "Enjoy your DVDs" from a "Robert T. Taylor." It turns out that "Robert Taylor" was monetizing the fact that U.S. TV series on DVDs sold for 30 dollars less in Germany than in Australia. When he received the order on eBay Australia he just entered the same order into Amazon.de, and asked Amazon.de to ship the box directly to the buyer in Singapore as a "gift." In the process he made a 30-dollar profit. I know about this story because the woman ordering the box of West Wing DVDs is my wife.

TAKE AWAY

The media companies of the world may try to keep control of when, where and how to distribute their content, but consumers are becoming more globally savvy and just want their stuff.

Are you still thinking borders, while your customers are letting go?

Human Needs
Why we need companies that focus on human needs.

SCENE: A CORNER OFFICE AT THE GLOBAL
OFFICE OF PHILIPS IN AMSTERDAM

When I met Antonio Hidalgo he held the positions Chief Innovation, Marketing and Strategy Officer for Philips Consumer Lifestyle and Head of Global Marketing for Philips. And even though he was in the middle of the rebranding of this 25-billion-dollar company, he still took time off to sit down with me for way over one hour to talk about how Philips is working on becoming a truly global company. He had just come back from a trip around the world where he had met with employees of Philips and asked them to tell him about what they were working on.

In our meeting Antonio spoke rapidly, energetically and passionately about the stories that they had told him. I hardly had time to ask questions as Antonio kept telling me story after story. When the clock showed that we had been sitting 30 minutes longer than our planned session, Antonio smiled and said, "I could be here until midnight telling you stories like this. And I would do it with pleasure!" I smiled back; it was obvious to me that he could.

In this chapter I will share some of the stories that he told me. I will then end by talking about what these stories told me about how Philips, as a brand and as a company, is transforming itself to a truly global company.

BACKGROUND

The first story Antonio shared with me was from the Middle East. Apparently breast cancer is a big problem in the region, partly because many women there, for cultural reasons, do not get screenings as often as in other regions. So Philips developed a truck, obviously only staffed with women, that drives into remote villages in the region to offer screenings. The trucks have new equipment that drastically reduces the radiation to the patient. (This was important since women used the fear of radiation as an excuse not to go for a check up.)

Antonio explained, "At Philips we care about people." In this story it was about getting more women to survive by finding cancer earlier.

The next two stories he told me were about how Philips used lighting technology to improve schools in Germany and the UK. By installing the right lighting system in a classroom, Philips could prove an 18% (!) increase in concentration in school kids in the UK. Similar figures came out of a test in a German school.

Antonio again, "This innovative solution has nothing to do with English or German school children. Every parent, and every principal, wants their children to get the best education possible. It is a universal need. A human need."

And just as he said that I realised the power in what he was saying. When they say, "We care about people," they mean it in the most fundamental and universal way, meaning: We care about human beings, human needs.

At first glance, that might seem too grand, too altruistic, too unspecific, or too general. But stop and think about it for a while, and you realize that it is actually a very focused, commercially viable and effective way of looking at what you do.

When Philips in Holland worked with a hospital to come up with a new solution of making it possible for premature babies and their mothers to recover by staying together (instead of having to be separated into different hospital departments), that is not a solution aimed at patients or health workers in Holland. Instead it is solving the universal need of mothers to be close to their babies after birth. Or as Antonio put it, "The solution is not for Dutch mothers, it is for mothers and their children wherever they may be. Indian mothers, American mothers, Thai mothers. Mothers, just mothers."

It is that last line, "Mothers, just mothers," that makes all the difference.

When Philips did a CSR project in Indonesia where it paid for chefs to come and cook affordable nutritious lunches for underprivileged school children with long commutes and school hours, it was, at its core, not a project about Indonesian school children, but a project to get children and schools interested in nutrition. To get them to want to eat better, to be healthier. A human need.

And when Philips is working with a local government in Germany to install street lamps that, thanks to its light, frequency and color reduces street violence (!), that is not -only- a solution for that city. It is a solution for the basic human emotion of feeling safe.

The more stories Antonio told me, the more fascinated I became with being reminded about how innovation and technology can be used to improve our lives. And the more inspired I became by how the ability to connect to basic human needs was driving Philips forward.

Antonio smiled (he does that a lot) and said, "We are a technology company that cares about people." And then he told me of yet another new product that they just had launched: The AirFryer.

The AirFryer is a machine that uses air to "deep fry" food (like french fries) by using much less oil than usual. By circulating the air at high speeds, it takes just a teaspoon of oil to make a serving of, say, french fries. The AirFryer was an innovation that came out of Europe, but by using its global R&D network, different teams around the world saw how the same technique could be used to make local dishes in Asia, India, China, Southeast Asia and other places. Local teams developed local accessories for local dishes to make it possible for more families to cook great tasting deep-fried food that is more healthy. A need that is not connected to Europe or Asia, or any other place in the world, but is universal.

It worked. And sales are, according to Antonio, "skyrocketing."

Antonio summarized our conversation, "We are at our best when we start with the user and look at how we can use innovation and technology to solve their problems and improve their lives. That makes us better listeners, more customer focused and better at producing innovation that matters." Then he added, "We are more global when we think like this! When you keep asking questions and go deeper, you finally come down to that fundamental human need. You stop thinking about developing a solution for a "French person" or a "Japanese woman" and instead you end up with a solution that is for "people" or "women."

I asked Antonio for some advice on how companies can become better at thinking about the human element of people, on how to go deep enough to connect with that universal, global, human level. He said, "Go to the extreme. Dig until you find that problem that you will solve which will be relevant to all. But don't expect that people will tell you what that deep desire is. That is our job to find."

Which brings us, in a way, back to where we started this story, on how Philips sends a truck full of the latest technology to the most remote villages in some of the world's most closed societies in order to help women in the Middle East overcome the stigma of having their breasts checked for cancer. A solution that, if it can work in an extreme situation like that, will give Philips insights that they can then use in the rest of the world in its pursuit of helping with the global wish of staying healthy.

TAKE AWAY

Is a company that defines itself as, for example, "an American car company" really best positioned to come up with solutions that will benefit humanity? Wouldn't a company defining itself as just "a car company" (or perhaps even better "a transportation company") be better positioned to be able to get deep down into the fundamental transportation needs that we all have?

The advantage of thinking like this is easy to see, but hard to do. I recently listened to a speech by Thomas Friedman in Singapore where he said something like, "I do not want the next generation of solar cells to be invented in China; I want them to be invented by American companies!"

I would have thought that he, the author of "The World is Flat," and a person who has traveled and written so much about the world would have a more global, human mindset. Personally, I just want a company to take the best people they can find in the world and make the best solar cell possible, to give us all better and more sustainable energy.

Antonio ended our conversation by mentioning a study he had read about how reading books was one of the best ways to reduce stress. But there was a twist to the study. Turns out it is not enough to just read any kind of book to reduce stress: It has to be a book that had some lessons in humanity. I think there is some very deep and fundamental truth in the message that Antonio gave to me. I hope you can see that, too.

What does your company do? I mean, when it really comes down to it. At a fundamental level, what human problem do you solve? And are you organized in a way that maximizes the benefit of what you do for humanity?

If not, why not?

Birds Without Borders
It pays to think big; just ask Angry Birds.

SCENE: HELSINKI, FINLAND

On a dark October day, I bumped into Peter Vesterbacka at the School of Art and Design at Aalto University in Helsinki, Finland. Both of us were invited to speak at the same conference. During a coffee break, I had the opportunity to interview him about his views on his company.

Peter Vesterbacka is the founder of Rovio, the company behind the game *Angry Birds*. The title on his business card reads "Mighty Eagle," and he attended the conference dressed in a bright red sweater designed after the big red bird from the game. He stood out in a crowd where most attendees were dressed in black and grey suits—obviously quite proud of his bird-slinging game. As he should be.

BACKGROUND

The success of *Angry Birds* is amazing. From a modest start in the end of 2009, the game just took off. In Spring 2011, less than 1.5 years after the game was launched, Wired wrote about the success, "Every day, users spend 200 million minutes—16 years every hour—playing the mobile game. Three trillion pigs have been popped. It has filled billions of those interstitial moments spent riding the bus, on a plane, or in important work meetings, and it is or has been the number one paid app on iTunes in 68 countries, as well as the best selling paid app of all time."

And it just keeps growing. On just one day—Christmas Day 2011—the game was downloaded 6.5 million times. As the game turned three years old, it passed 500 million downloads. That's on a planet with 7 billion people. Those cute little birds are now leaving the mobile screen and can be seen everywhere, from advertising campaigns for Finnair, to give-away prices at the Singapore Airport to Angry Birds bags in small street corner shops in China.

But Peter is not done. They just passed the one billion download mark. Peter talked seriously about kicking Disney off the throne. Considering that Rovio was able to sell ten million stuffed Angry Birds toys in its first year (not counting the estimated 80 million(!) fake ones sold during the same period), it doesn't seem totally unlikely.

I asked Peter, "Are you a Finnish company?" He shook his head and said, "Nighty-eight percent of the people who work for Rovio are in Finland, but that is irrelevant." When invited to speak to a crowd of Finnish businessmen as an example of a "successful Finnish company," Peter explained that he doesn't want people to know the company is located in Finland.

"We want to be more American than apple pie in the U.S. and more Chinese than moon cake in China," he said. Rovio has released different versions of the game for different markets, and promotes it differently with, for example, a Year of the Dragon animation in celebration of the Chinese New Year. (The two-and-a-half minute animation got 9.3 million views on YouTube in one month.)

Rovio thinks, acts and behaves as if *Angry Birds* is a global product, and perhaps that is one of the reasons it is.

On its website under the heading "Who We Are," the company writes, "Rovio is an entertainment media company, and the creator of the globally successful Angry Birds franchise." (Further down in the text they do state, "Rovio's headquarters are located in Finland.") But they do not write, "Rovio is a Finnish entertainment media company." It is, as Peter started out by saying to me, "irrelevant."

TAKE AWAY

Ask yourself this question: If Rovio would have identified themselves as an "Finnish entertainment media company," do you think it is more or less likely that they would have achieved the same rapid, unprecedented domination in such a short period of time?

When you describe your company, how do you describe it? Do you put the country of the founder in the description? If so, why?

Notes

"One world, one company, one network" DACHSER GMBH & CO. KG

We Are the World
What penguins can teach us about being human.

SCENE: HOME OF THE PENGUINS

There are always two sides to a story. Every company that I have interviewed for this book can be said to have a long way to go before they are a global company. At the same time, they have all come far on the journey to become one.

The paint company Jotun is a perfect example of this. In one way, they are a very Norwegian company—owned for three generations by the Gleditsch family of the small Norwegian fishing village of Sandefjord, where the company was founded and is still headquartered. On the other hand, Jotun is a global company consisting of 74 companies and 39 production facilities on all continents, with a presence in 80 countries and with a second headquarters in Dubai.

I sat down with Björn Naglestad, general manager of Jotun China, to talk about how the company was making the transition into performing as a global company.

BACKGROUND

Björn is Norwegian. Very Norwegian. He is happy, positive and friendly in that natural way so many Norwegians seem to be. But the first thing he said to me was, "*We* are not Norwegian. *I* am Norwegian, but *the company* is not." I asked him what Jotun was if they were not Norwegian. He broke out in a huge smile and said, "We are penguins!"

Let me explain.

The current logo of Jotun shows a small penguin embracing the Earth. The original logo, however, was a picture of the hammer of Thor, the god of thunder in Nordic mythology. It's symbolic of how the symbol of the company has gone from local to global.

When Björn says, "We are penguins!" he means it. "We sing penguin songs; we preach penguin culture," he said. Björn described how he looks at his role as manager in China, "I am not here to teach the Chinese to sell paint to the Chinese. I am here to preach culture." Or as Björn put it, "Anyone can be a penguin. Not anyone can be Norwegian. We are here to build culture and we cannot build a culture around a minority [the Norwegians]."

Out of 8,000 employees, about 1,500 are in China and another 1,000 are in Southeast Asia. Only about 15 of them are expats. All of them are penguins.

To be a penguin means to subscribe to the corporate values of Jotun, no matter what passport you hold. The company has a few absolutes that everyone has to sign up for, and their values are very strong. These values are: Loyalty, care, respect and boldness.

Björn told me a story about how the values—in this case, "care" and "loyalty"—drive the company. In China, Jotun had been able to recruit a young female CFO who had graduated number one in her class from one of Shanghai's best universities. Then unexpectedly she was diagnosed with cancer. She came to Björn's office and wanted to resign so she could focus on getting well. Björn told her, "If you work two minutes per day, I will pay you full salary." The women asked why he would do this, and Björn replied, "I want you to feel that we miss you and that you have a job to come back to when you are not sick anymore."

The woman fought her cancer and became well again, and she

still works for the company. Interesting fact: In China, Jotun has a turnover rate of just six (!) percent. Loyalty goes both ways.

During the Shanghai World Expo, Jotun had a huge gathering for employees, customers and partners in China. But they did not have it in the Norwegian pavilion. Björn looked almost insulted that I had assumed that's where they'd held their event. "Are you mad? Of course we were not in the Norwegian pavilion! Nor the Dubai pavilion [where the other headquarters of Jotun is]. We needed a bigger place!" He laughed. Jotun had leased the Chinese Cultural Hall for their event, where 7,500 people attended a concert and 1,500 Penguins were the VIPs. Jotun treated the World Expo as a fair for the world, not as an exhibition for a bunch of countries.

According to Björn, referring to everyone as "penguins" creates equality with everyone. The employees become "a little bit less Chinese" and a "little bit less Norwegian" when they are at work. Instead they "become a little bit more penguin," which of course is code for everyone becoming a little bit more human. Björn ended his description of how the company treats its employees by saying, "We are motivated by the same issues; we cry and laugh for the same reasons. Penguins are the same all over the world."

TAKE AWAY

Björn Naglestad's last quote reminded me of a passage I read in the book *"The Michael Jackson Tapes,"* which consists of conversations between the famous singer and Rabbi Shmuley Boteach. Much can be said about Michael Jackson, but few can criticize his skills as a performer and his ability to connect to a crowd. In the book, Michael said, "We are all the same, and I have the perfect hypothesis to prove it. I play to all those countries and they cry in the same place in my show. They laugh in the same places.

They become hysterical in the same places. They faint in the same places. [...] I have heard that the Russians are hard-nosed and the Germans have no feelings and emotions [but] they were just as emotional [at my concerts as anyone else]."

Jackson's observation about us as humans is worth taking note of. We are less different than we think. And a company that is able to make its employees feel equal, instead of different, is a company that will have committed employees with common goals and values.

So let's learn from the man who sang, "We Are The World" and "I'm Not Gonna Spend My Life Being A Color." Let's be less nationalistic, and more human.

Experts vs Expats

When the processes and procedures are not keeping up.

SCENE: THE AUSTRALIAN CLUB IN MELBOURNE

The research for this chapter began during a lunch conversation at The Australian Club in Melbourne. This classic gentleman's club was established in 1878. A monument to a time gone past, the club would turn out to be a fitting environment to talk about how some companies are using antiquated and outdated HR practices in today's world, while others are moving with the times.

BACKGROUND

The man I had lunch with asked not to be named in this book, but he used to work for a company that calls itself "global" but in its processes still behaves very much as a French company. One example: the HR department had specified that managers had to fly economy class one way and business class going back. This was based on the fact that French managers flew to the U.S. on day flights and flew back on night flights. The business class rule was there to let the French managers sleep in the business-class bed at night. But if you fly between France and Australia, you are bound to have a night flight for some part of your trip. However, my Australian friend was only allowed a business class ticket one way, since the HR department had not considered the flight times from Australia. The rules should have been "If you fly during the night you can fly business," not "A flight in one direction can be business."

The same man also told me that the company has decided that if a French manager moved abroad to Houston, for example, he would get an expat package. But if a manager from Houston moved to France, no such package would be paid out. The company even set a rule that a certain percentage of the staff should be French.

The story reminded me of my biggest disappointment while researching this book. I had booked an interview with *"Doctors Without Borders"* because I imagined that an organization with a name like that would be experts in behaving as a borderless organization. I turned out to be totally wrong. Doctors Without Borders is a very "French" organization, run and controlled from France—and doctors in Doctors Without Borders even have expat salaries!

Read that again: Doctors in Doctors Without Borders have expat salaries…

A global company should not have "expat" salaries. It should have "expert" salaries. A company should pay a higher salary to someone because that person is an expert, not because that person comes from another country. By changing the wording from "expat" salary to "expert" salary, you send the message that people with higher salaries are getting them because they are experts—not because they are from another country.

Actually, a global company should have no rules or regulations to support a specific nationality, unless those rules are there to make it easier for under-represented nationalities to get the same chance as everyone else.

TAKE AWAY

The Australian Club was founded at a time when it was considered wise to hire only men into senior positions, thus the rule at the time that only men could enter this gentleman's club. Today women are also allowed into The Australian Club. Times have changed, but a lot of companies still struggle to hire women into top positions. Companies that *do* hire women to fill senior positions have realized the advantage of picking the best from a larger pool of professionals. In the same way, some companies are now realizing the potential of searching the whole world for the best talents instead of picking people only from a specific country.

Are processes and procedures helping your company make the transition to a global company—or holding it back?

Notes

"One world. One company. One goal of communicating better." ENTEL SYSTEMS, INC.

At 30,000 ft you see no borders

About what happens when an airline thinks outside the (border)lines.

SCENE: THE EMIRATES HEADQUARTERS NEXT TO THE AIRPORT IN DUBAI

Just a few minutes after I stepped off my Emirates flight from Singapore and walked through the huge new airport of Dubai, I entered the head office of Emirates for a meeting with Georgette Kolkman. I wanted to learn how an airline can excel in thinking globally.

Before we jump into this chapter, let me ask you a question: How many different nationalities do you think work for Emirates? Do you have a number in your head? Whatever that number is, I am going to stick my neck out and say that number is too low.

BACKGROUND

So how many different nationalities did you think Emirates has working for them?

The correct number is 167!

Yes, one hundred and sixty seven different nationalities — in an industry that traditionally prides itself on boasting about its home roots and that likes to play on nationalistic strings.

"We have a different mindset," says Georgette Kolkman. Emirates is less busy looking at how the landscape of a nationalistic airline industry used to look, and more focused on where the travel industry is heading. So, where is it heading?

Georgette Kolkman explains, "The world has changed. The Internet changed the way people travel; it created a different kind of travel. More people live in a borderless world. They have traveled so much more than before. We have a new class of traveler who has what we call 'the globalista mindset.'" Then she adds, "We exist to connect globalistas and inspire the new world." What they call "globalistas" is a rapidly growing group who travel the world for more reasons than just business or leisure. The kind of people who will fly in to Singapore to attend the F1 race; the business person who flies into London for a few meetings over the day; the retired couple who spends a year traveling around the world. The visiting friends and relatives. As more people migrate to other parts of the world, this rapidly growing group looks at the world, and at traveling, in a different way.

The corporate slogan of Emirates is "Hello Tomorrow." It's a bold statement, but the more I hear Georgette speak about how Emirates is run, the more fitting I find it. Emirates is not built around yesterday, but around what the world is going to look like tomorrow. Georgette explained, "Our slogan is a greeting to what the future has to offer. We are inventing tomorrow; we are inventing the future of travel. The world is more connected than we think."

The way that Emirates is run goes much deeper than a slogan, which brings us back to that amazing number of 167 different nationalities working for the company—and to what that means.

Georgette Kolkman tells me how she can sit in a meeting with colleagues of ten to fifteen different nationalities, and how the group dynamics change when no nationality or nationalistic culture dominates a meeting. I ask her how this changes the way they work. She replies, "First of all, your decision making gets sharper. When you have people looking at things from different ways, you get more focused (on the best idea). When you get consensus in that kind of environment, then you know you have an idea that has been looked at from all viewpoints. It makes the ideas stronger."

I ask her what other advantages there are in working in such a diverse corporate culture, and she says, "When you are many people with different ideas of how things should be done, you need to argue why you think your way is the best. In a climate like that, different ideas compete against each other, and they compete on their merits, not on history or heritage."

She stops for a while to let me finish my note taking so I can focus on what she will say next, "Here, nothing is 'good because we used to do it like that.' Here we 'do it because it is good.'"

I just love the power of that statement.

Georgette then likens an organization to a person by saying, "As a person, you are the sum of the places you've been and the people you have met. It is what makes you who you are. What we are trying to do (as an organization) is to celebrate the wide variety of experiences inside our company. To appreciate the different cultures that we have."

According to Georgette, this way of thinking has created a corporate culture that is fast, innovative, and adaptive to change. And she admits that is not a culture for everyone. "You either stay here for six months or forever," she says, and then adds that she herself has been with the organization for 17 years. She obviously likes it, and when I ask her why she has stayed so long, she says, "Once you get past the shock of working in such a diverse culture and you allow yourself to embrace it, it's so exciting!"

It seems to be working. The airline has averaged more than 20 percent annual growth since its birth in 1985. In 2011/2012 they flew 34 million passengers, up from 27 million in 2009/2011. They now fly to more than 130 cities in 76 countries on six continents. Moreover, the company has enjoyed continuous profitability year on year, which is almost unique in an industry famous for losing money.

In a world where the nationality of the airline is becoming less important for global travelers, many airlines still try to think of themselves as connected to a specific country. When I ask Georgette why other airlines seem stuck on thinking in the context of "home country," instead of focusing on building a world class company, with a world class brand that anyone can connect to, she bursts out in laughter and says, "I have no idea! I do not understand their mentality or logic! By thinking like that, they are constraining their own growth. It is like they do not want their world to change. But the world is changing. You cannot be an international nationalistic airline (anymore). If you don't realize this, you've missed the train…"

We both laugh at her choice of a train as metaphor for the airline industry.

TAKE AWAY

After our meeting, I walk back to Dubai Airport and board an Emirates plane to Pakistan. As we taxi out to the runway, I look around at the diverse backgrounds of passengers on the plane. A friendly voice on the intercom says, "Welcome aboard this Emirates flight to Karachi. On this flight, our crew speaks English, Arabic, Hindi, Urdu, Punjabi, German, Swahili, Mandarin, French, Swedish, and Thai." It becomes so obvious how outdated it is to run a company based on the location of its headquarters. And how fresh and forward looking it feels to view the world as your home. Especially, but not exclusively, for an airline.

Taking a global approach to your business is not easy. It will create tension, conflict, and perhaps even more work. But if you get it to work, it will elevate you to the next level. Which company is the "Emirates" in your industry? Who has decided to leave the nationalistic thinking behind, to get the best people they can, to create the best customer experience possible—no matter what passport that customer might hold?

Is it just a coincidence that the most globally organized airline is also one of the fastest growing and most profitable airlines in the world? Would you become more productive and innovative if you built into your DNA that the best ideas have to fight against each other—instead of thinking that some ideas are better because they come from the same country as the flag on the tail wing of your company?

Notes

One World. 152,000 people. One network.

When your customer tells you to go global, you better pay attention.

SCENE: KPMG ASIA PACIFIC PARTNER CONFERENCE IN SYDNEY, AUSTRALIA

If there were a defining moment when I realized the time had arrived for me to write this book, it would be when I was invited to the KPMG Asia Pacific Partner Conference in Sydney, Australia. Together with more than 500 partners and senior employees, I listened to Michael Andrew, the newly appointed Chairman of KPMG International, spell out the new global strategy of this 152,000-person professional services network.

BACKGROUND

Sitting in the back of the Sydney Four Seasons Hotel ballroom, I listened as the Global Chairman set out the key areas where the network was prioritizing. Now, "being global" is nothing new in business or to KPMG, of course, as indicated by something Michael Andrew pointed out in his speech. "This is the fourth global strategy that we have launched," he said. The previous three had all succumbed, to some extent, to a lack of global implementation. He looked out over the crowd, and added, "But this time it is different."

You can be sure that I was paying attention to what he said next.

Michael Andrew clarified how it was different this time. His answer, in short, was "clients." He explained that KPMG had completed a brand review where, among other things, they had asked their clients this question: "What do you think KPMG stands for when we are at our best?"

The key words their clients came back with were:

Global mindset

Forward thinking

Passionate

Expert

Value adding

Let me stress this: Their clients were saying to KPMG that one of the things they valued most about KPMG member firms was to have "a global mindset!' Being global for KPMG isn't about structure – far from it. It's about mindset and being relevant to their clients.

I asked Rachel Campbell, Global Head of People Performance and Culture, if "having a global mindset" was something that had always been on the list of the top five things their customers appreciated with KPMG. She thought about the question for a moment, and said, "No, I do not think it would have been there so consistently across our clients five years ago."

Something had clearly changed in the last few years. Global mindset was not just some buzzword floating around; it was one of the qualities their clients prioritized most of all. This time it really seemed to be different. Companies have now decided they want suppliers who understand and know how to operate in a world that is globally connected. For big companies, this is important because they want a professional services firm that can service them professionally in all the locations where they do business. But, it is also important for the smaller, more local clients of KPMG member firms who come to the firms wanting "the best ideas from around the world."

And when your client tells you to go global, you better pay attention.

That is exactly what KPMG is doing.

At one of the panel discussions later in the day, one panelist said, "We are organizing ourselves to align with the way our clients are structuring their business." Today that means being more global in our approach.

I learned a lot about being global during the conference. Some of the things I learned were too confidential for me to share. But here are some of the key take aways about how KPMG is putting action behind the phrase of having a global mindset.

1) Location of the Global Chairman's Office.

How about this for a start: Following the announcement of Michael Andrew as the new Global Chairman, there was another announcement. The Global Chairman's office would no longer be in New York but in Hong Kong. A network with 152,000 people decided it was appropriate to have their Global Chairman's office in Asia because it is closer to the high growth markets of Asia. Before his promotion to Global Chairman, Michael Andrew was Chairman of the KPMG Asia Pacific region, as well as of KPMG Australia. For him, it was both practical and strategic to place the Global Chairman's office in Asia—and in a truly global network, people working in international roles are not connected to one specific place.

KPMG did not originate from "one place." Rather, as the many letters in its name suggest, the network originated as a result of a long series of mergers by accounting companies in the UK, Germany, Holland, United States and other countries. This process of consolidation had been ongoing for over 100 years. Member firms of the KPMG network are separate and legally distinct, and each firm is affiliated with KPMG International Cooperative, a Swiss entity registered in the Swiss Canton of Zug.

A network of member firms located in 156 countries with an Australian Global Chairman based in Asia truly communicates both internally and externally that KPMG is committed to having a global mindset.

2) The Global Executive Team.

The Global Executive Team includes representatives from Hong Kong, Germany, United States, Japan, China, Brazil, France and the Netherlands. As appropriate, the team coordinates their meeting schedule with meetings held by regional KPMG leadership teams. This is especially beneficial as the local and regional partners have the opportunity to engage with global leadership on a more frequent basis.

3) Real resources behind the talk.

If you are going to be serving global clients, it is not enough to simply talk about having a global mindset. You need to make sure you are investing enough time and resources behind it. Perhaps the lack of commitment was one of the reasons that previous global strategies at KPMG failed. One of the people I spoke with at the KPMG conference was Mark Britnell, Global Head of Healthcare for KPMG. He explained that in the past he was a part time "Global Head of Healthcare.'" As he insightfully put it, "How could I make a difference?" Obviously, he couldn't — "Global Head of Healthcare" was just an empty phrase. Today he is working full time as Global Head of Healthcare, flying around the world helping KPMG member firms acquire the best knowledge, resources, information and competencies from around the world to solve their clients' health care issues.

4) Don't centralize. Globalize.

Being a global network does not mean having a huge headcount in a single location. KPMG is perfect proof of that. With 152,000 people in member firms worldwide, the total number working in Hong Kong full time for the Global Chairman's office is just ten.

As Rachel Campbell, KPMG Global Head of People Performance and Culture, explained: "People confuse 'global' with being 'centralized,' "which is a *big* mistake." To stress how big a mistake, she dragged out the word big to a "biiiiiiiiigggggg mistake."

Rachel also explained how important she thought it was for HR to be part of any central strategy, saying, "When I hear [HR people] talk about how HR is 'aligned with the strategy,' I become very frustrated! HR has to be an integral *part* of the strategy." In the case of HR (or as KPMG calls it, "People Performance and Culture"), their role is to make sure that having a global mindset really means something for their people.

There is, remarked Rachel, a difference between "diverse" and "inclusive." A diverse company that is not inclusive will look good on paper but will not work. An inclusive company will automatically become a diverse one. To successfully run a global company, there has to be a culture where people are willing to be inclusive of others who are, for whatever reason (race, nationality, age, gender, hair color, hobbies, and so forth), not like them. A global company is not a company where everyone is the same. It is a company where everyone is willing to work together.

Rachel Campbell summed up her thoughts: "We do not worry so much about national boundaries anymore." Then she corrected herself, perhaps realizing the dangers of complacency and added, "We do, though, still need to do more than 'think global.'" Clearly, KPMG has not reached its final destination, but they have come far along the journey.

TAKE AWAY

KPMG is one of the "big four" global professional services networks. One way they keep growing is by acquiring good local accounting firms that are, as the Global Chairman put it, "trapped in a country." KPMG still has the power of local knowledge, but it also has the power of a global network that is, literally, able to find the best resources in the world to give the best advice to its clients. Nevertheless, KPMG did not reach this position by chance. A company that does not invest in creating a global mindset will not harvest the benefits it creates. How much concrete effort is your company putting behind its words?

Non-nationalistic Companies
When companies migrate to the world.

SCENE: THE EARTH

If companies move up a level and start identifying themselves not as "companies from a country" but as "companies in the world," and if corporate leaders start making decisions primarily out of concern of their company, not the country that their company comes from, what will the result be?

BACKGROUND

In the month prior to the Summer Olympics in Beijing in 2008, the Chinese hosts organized the longest torch relay in the history of the games. When the *Journey of Harmony*, as it was called, came to Paris, the Chinese had decided to have a woman in a wheelchair from the Chinese Paralympic team carry the torch. While wheeling the torch down the streets of Paris, she was attacked by angry pro-Tibetan protesters. The incident generated an outrage among netizens in China, with many calling for the boycott of "French companies" such as retailer Carrefour. Carrefour quickly issued a statement saying that the company supported the Beijing Olympics, and that they would "never do anything to harm the feelings of Chinese people." Why this reaction? Perhaps because Carrefour has over 200 hypermarkets in China. On its website the company writes:

"A pioneering entrant in countries such as Brazil (1975) and China (1995), the group currently operates in three major markets: Europe, Latin America and Asia. With a presence in 32 countries, over 57% of group turnover derives from outside France. The group sees strong potential for further international growth in the future, particularly in such large national markets as China, Brazil, Indonesia, Poland and Turkey."

As the world's second largest retailer, with almost half a million employees, sees the potential for future growth outside France, the incentive to be identified as a "French retailer" becomes less and less intriguing. In a world of conflicts and high emotions between nations, companies like Carrefour benefit from distancing themselves from countries and defining themselves around the service they deliver. Carrefour is a retailer—not a "French retailer."

Another example of what happens when a company lets go of the nationalistic identification was recently described in a fascinating article in Wired Magazine. In a story that read like a script of an action movie from Hollywood, Wired described how the "Stuxnet" computer worm infected computers in Iranian nuclear facilities. Experts from the data security company Symantec worked on identifying and neutralizing the worm that had infected Siemens computers in Iran. Here was a bunch of Symantec employees, in different offices around the world, fighting the Stuxnet worm even as the researchers risked tampering with what could have been a covert U.S. government operation.

In the article, a Symantec employee is asked if they were concerned about this. The article read, "Chien [the Symantec employee] replied, 'For us there's no good guys or bad guys.' Then he paused to reconsider. 'Well, bad guys are people who are writing malicious code that infects systems, that can cause unintended consequences or intended consequences.'"

Whether the "bad guy" was the United States or one of its allies, the attack was causing collateral damage to thousands of systems, and Symantec felt no patriotic duty to preserve its activity. "We're not beholden to a nation," Chien said. "We're a multinational private company protecting customers."

Computer safety experts who are not beholden to a nation. Who put their loyalty first and foremost to their employee and to solving their customers' problems. Companies and their employees are clearly leaving "country" as their primary means of identification and moving up a level.

Our third example is about what happens if the unions also start to think in global terms. Recently a Swedish union representative named Lars-Anders Häggström talked about IKEA. He said, "If a company has a strategy that all IKEA stores should have the same concepts, the same look and feel, even the same meatballs in the restaurants worldwide, then shouldn't they have the same policy in regard to unions and workers' rights?" Interesting idea. If people start to identify themselves more with the company they work for than the country they live in, will this create a global workers' union demanding the same rights, same benefits, and same quality of life regardless of what country they happen to work in?

Companies distancing themselves from countries, employees putting their loyalty first and foremost to their company instead of their country, union leaders talking of solidarity amongst workers for one company worldwide, instead of loyalty for workers in one country.

Where will the journey towards truly global companies take us? It is a question as difficult to answer as it is intriguing to ask. One thing is clear: Countries will become weaker. When business leaders and organizations stop identifying themselves with one country, politicians lose a previously strong and loyal ally—an ally that most politicians still do not understand that they have lost. I have interviewed numerous business leaders who have described how they now take no consideration—none whatsoever!—their company's former home country when taking strategic business decisions. So the companies have moved on while the politicians still talk, behave—and make decisions—as if the companies are still "theirs." It is like the girl who thinks she's still in a relationship, when the truth is that the boy has already broken up with her and moved on. Not a very nice position to be in.

TAKE AWAY

The theme of the 2008 Olympic games was "One world, One dream." That is a slogan perhaps more suitable for globally minded individuals and organizations than for a bunch of countries. When change happens, things change. The rise of truly global companies is going to change the world in more ways than most people understand. What changes do you see happening?

One Social Planet

Facebook grows around people, not around countries.

SCENE: IN THE CORRIDORS OF THE HR SUMMIT

Madan Nagaldinne is head of HR for Facebook in Asia. He and I happened to speak at the same HR conference earlier this year. After listening to his presentation about how Facebook looks at HR, I went up to him and told him that I was writing a book about global companies, and that I wished to discuss the subject with him. He began by saying, "It's one world. You have to be one company."

I smiled and told him that the title of the book I was writing was *"One World. One Company."* … He took two steps back and threw his hands up in the air, "WOW! I didn't know that. We have to talk!" So right there and then we began a conversation about how Facebook looks at the world.

BACKGROUND

Everyone knows how big Facebook, the service, is, but few know how small Facebook, the company, is. When I write this, the company has so many members that, if it were a country, it would easily be the third largest country in the world. They have one billion members, but the company has less than 4,000 employees. (That's about 250,000 users per employee…)

Facebook might be bigger than all countries in the world except India and China, but Facebook is not a country. They do not think along the lines of countries, borders or nationalities. They think about people and the connections between them.

That makes a lot of sense. Creativity is the ability to connect the unconnected.

Innovation comes when you connect the right people and the right ideas.

As a Facebook user, you know how the service connects you with your friends, no matter where in the world they happen to be at the moment. Now, imagine the same close and borderless connection between the people in your organization.

Madan Nagaldinne has worked in many other companies, but he is convinced that Facebook is run differently, and that one of the reasons for its success is that Facebook was founded in the 21st century—and that the company has taken maximum advantage of how changes in technology have opened up new possibilities for how to run a company.

Madan began telling me about how Facebook, the company, runs its operations.

Facebook is constantly "fighting to stay small," and regardless if you are a programmer or something else, you are expected to be, in the words of Facebook, "a hacker." Now, a hacker is not someone who tries to break into someone else's IT system. Madan described it like this, "We are hackers. We solve problems by bringing people together really fast."

He gave a few examples of what that could mean:

A group of just a few people decided to build a way to send personal videos to your friends and started hacking away. After 40 straight hours of work, they had a functional feature that they sent out for testing. Shortly thereafter, this same feature was rolled out on the whole network and used by hundreds of millions of users.

The HR department realized they needed a process on how to check for culture while recruiting. A small team, across borders and across functions, sat down and developed a set of questions. In ten hours, they had the new process up and running in Asia. Shortly after that, it was implemented around the world.

Madan explained that one way the company is able to stay so small (and quick) is that they make sure that they utilize the competencies in the whole organization globally in order to solve a problem, instead of having redundant competencies in different regions or countries. And he gives the example of how HR in Asia used an HR executive in another part of the world to handle an recruitment because the HR department in Asia did not have time. He summarized it as, "Global teams at Facebook work with global opportunities."

Not only does this make the organization very "fat free," it also has an added another benefit according to Madan. "If you get the best [suited] designer, who happens to sit in Latin America; the best programmer, who happens to sit in Palo Alto; and the best project manager, who happens to sit in Singapore, to work together on a project, you not only get the best product in the world—you also include diversity in the product."

I found that last statement extremely insightful, "You also include diversity in the product."

I asked him how this new way of thinking is different from how other companies are run. "[In the previous companies I worked] before, you had barriers. It was one dimensional. Now you get a totally different kind of innovation. It is not two dimensional - it is multidimensional."

Think about it. Who will be most innovative: The company that connects the best people—and the best ideas—whoever and wherever they may be—or the company that connects only the ones who are in the same country?

TAKE AWAY

Henry Ford became successful by taking advantage of new technology to launch a new kind of product. A big part of the success came from Ford's ability to embrace new technologies to change the way its organization was organized.

It is called "Fordism," and has been defined as, "A manufacturing philosophy that aims to achieve higher productivity by standardizing the output, using conveyor assembly lines, and breaking the work into small deskilled tasks."

Perhaps in the future we will talk about Mark Zuckerberg as our times' Henry Ford. Facebook not only introduced a new technology to the masses, the company also embraced how changes in technology made it possible to change the way we today could organize our organizations.

Lets call it "Facebookism," and define it as, "An organizational philosophy that aims to achieve higher productivity by increasing the connections between people and breaking down barriers to make it possible for small teams to work together on their task in a decentralized, diverse, and free way."

Madan ended our chat by saying, "There is an amazing potential to increase productivity and efficiency [by working like this] and it will interrupt the way we work." For Madan Nagaldinne and the rest of the employees at Facebook, it already has. For you?

Cognizant

*How small things make the world smaller
—and create massive growth.*

SCENE: A DINNER TABLE AT THE SHANGRI-LA HOTEL BALLROOM IN SINGAPORE

Gordon Coburn stepped right off a 20-hour flight from the U.S. into a full day event for Cognizant's most important customers in Southeast Asia. At the dinner that followed he was still full of energy, and I got a chance to sit down and interview him about how the company that he is president of looks at the concept of One World, One Company.

BACKGROUND

I had been the keynote speaker at the conference earlier that day, where Gordon also had delivered a company presentation. Company presentations can be very boring, but Gordon spoke passionately about Cognizant in a highly likable style that I can only describe as "humble bragging."

At the dinner I started by asking Gordon about the theme of this book, "Is Cognizant a TGC—a Truly Global Company?"

He replied, "We were born with a global DNA." He then explained how, because of its unique founding history, Cognizant had been well positioned to become a truly global company. Cognizant was originally founded as an in-house technology unit of The Dun & Bradstreet Corporation back in 1994 to jump-start its operations in India. At the time they had 200 employees, almost all of them in India. Within a couple of years of its founding, the company began adding third-party clients and servicing multiple industry segments. It is now a full-fledged IT and consulting company. The company is headquartered in the U.S., but around three-quarters of its employees are based in India. Even today many people in the U.S. look at Cognizant as an "Indian company," while many people in India look at it as an "American company." But inside Cognizant they just look at it as "a global company," with over 50 delivery centers worldwide and more than 150,000 employees spread across five continents.

When I asked him to give me an example of what being a global company means to them, Gordon mentioned how they had organized their teams, "At Cognizant, teams are not built around locations; teams are built around helping clients build stronger businesses. Geography is irrelevant." He also emphasized how they work hard to implement processes in the company so that everyone knows how things should be done, since geographic distances otherwise risk making teamwork harder. "It's easy when everyone on a team works in the same building, and you can walk over and say 'Hey, Steve, about this problem...' You cannot do that when people are sitting around the world. And we still need to act like ONE."

That sounds all good and well, but I wanted to have a more concrete example of what they had done. Some simple thing that other companies could learn from. Gordon understood what I wanted, and said, "We are *big* users of teleconferencing!" I think he could see that I was skeptical, so he added, "It [video conferences] changed us massively." When I heard him describe how using video conferences had improved their teamwork across different locations, I realized that sometimes leadership is those small, practical things, like getting people to actually use video conferences, and making sure the technology is good enough, easily available, and easy to use. By being able to "see" the other members of your team, regardless where they sit, you build trust between team members, and teams that trust each other work better together.

What I really liked was how the top management had made an effort to get everyone to embrace the video technology—because if technology is not being used, it is of no use. Gordon told me that when they introduced the idea of using more video conferences, both the CEO and the COO declared that they would not take any phone calls with any managers. If someone wanted to talk to them, they had to do it using telepresence.

They used the same "common sense" approach for their big video broadcasted "town hall meetings." (Or I guess they should be called "planet hall meetings," since they include people from all around the world.) When they book the meetings, they calculate what the optimal time to broadcast it would be, based on when it will be the least inconvenient for the most people to attend. If that meant the CEO had to make his speech at 11:30 PM (his time), so be it. Apparently it took a while to get the admin staff to learn to schedule according to the time zones of the audience instead of when it would be most convenient for the CEO, but now it comes naturally to how they think.

"Small things like this make a huge difference. You are sending out a message that you understand that people are really sitting around the world. As a leader, you send out a message that the world is not revolving around you, but that you understand that the world is revolving," said Gordon. He added, "Change management is not a huge project; it can also be changing the way you do things yourself. People will not do what their boss tells them unless the boss also shows that he or she will play by the same rules."

The more I listened to Gordon, the more I was reminded of the importance for a leader to focus on the small symbolic things, not just the big strategic decisions. "Use video conferencing" may sound like simplified advice on how to become a global company, but if that is how you interpret the message from Gordon, you are missing the point.

Frankly, any business leader who is interested in growth should listen carefully to what a company like Cognizant is doing. Remember how I started this chapter by talking about how Gordon Coburn had been "humbly bragging?" Well, unless you are familiar with Cognizant, pay attention. Here are some of the facts that he presented:

Less than 20 years after it was founded, the company already has well over 150,000 employees. Just in 2011, they grew by 35,000 people. Gordon likened that to adding another 20 employees per hour—every hour—for a full year. The company has made the "Fast Tech 25" list for a record ten years in a row, and it was one of the fastest companies in the history to go from joining the Forbes 1,000 to joining the Fortune 500.

That is impressive growth, but a lot of companies have grown fast. What really fascinated me was how the company had been able to grow so quickly while at the same time keeping its quality. This year, they had a 72% employee satisfaction rate (which is "off the chart" for IT companies) and an 87% customer satisfaction rate (also among the highest in the industry). And they have among the lowest employee turnover ratios in the industry. They did all that while keeping the company debt free. They actually have 2.3 billion dollar in cash in the bank. No wonder that Gordon, in his previous role as CFO, was voted "one of the best CFOs in the U.S." for six years running.

Gordon Coburn, who has been with the company since 1996, had a very relaxed and frank way of describing the remarkable rapid expansion. He said, "Employees and customers who like the company, stay—and that means growth."

My follow-up question was, "Did you grow so fast because you are global, or are you global because you grew so fast?"

He said, "It's a little bit of both. But it is clear that if we didn't act as a global company, we would not have grown so quickly."

TAKE AWAY

The rapid growth of Cognizant around the world is inspiring. But the most valuable take away from my dinner interview with Cognizant's president was the need for leaders to act in a way that makes the rest of the organization feel that all this talk about acting as "one" and behaving as a truly global company, is not just talk.

Notes

"One world. One company. One passion. One Sight." LUXOTTICA GROUP

"Made by..." vs "Made in..."
Why it is more relevant to talk about who made a product, than where it was made.

SCENE: A BAR IN HONG KONG HARBOUR

When the employees and distributors of SPI (owners of Stolichnaya Premium Vodka) were done with the day-program of their global conference they continued to a bar. Not too surprising: They make vodka after all. Sitting next to a Russian woman working for the company we started to talk about vodka, Russia and Stolichnaya. Her answers might surprise some, but let's start with some background.

BACKGROUND

Stolichnaya is a typical example of how a company can transition from "country-origin" to "value-origin." Stolichnaya was created at the beginning of the 1900s (no one really knows for sure) in Russia, and for the longest time the product branded itself as "Russian vodka." But, with the fall of the Soviet Union, the distillery in Riga ended up not being in Russia anymore, but in Latvia. In the beginning of 2010, the owners of Stolichnaya Vodka decided to rebrand it and call it Premium vodka instead of Russian vodka. This coincided with the Russian legislative changes making it illegal to export bulk vodka (i.e. in large tanks) from Russia. Stolichnaya has been bottled in Riga since 1948. SPI/Stolichnaya now export from their distillery in Tambov (Russia) the highest grade of raw alcohol (the key ingredient in vodka), called Alpha spirit, rather than finished Russian vodka.

So is Stolichnaya Russian vodka or Latvian vodka?

A tricky question that Stolichnaya has chosen to answer by rewriting the question.

Because though SPI/Stolichnaya is still very proud of its heritage and the Russian origin of its ingredients, it is no longer primarily branding its vodka based on country, but on brand values and product quality. In 2012 they launched a new global advertising campaign with the slogan: "The most original people deserve the most original vodka." "Stoli," as the product is affectionately called, is now less about where it comes from, and more about what kind of person drinks it.

For the company, the rebranding of Stoli coincided with a shake-up within the company, where it went from being a primary Russian organization to a truly global organization. In 2008, Pernod Ricard, the company that had distributed Stoli globally, bought Absolut Vodka. Suddenly they had their own vodka brand, which created a conflict of interest: Pernod was not allowed to distribute both brands. SPI/Stoli found themselves with a lot of vodka, but no one to distribute it. In a few months they were forced to entirely rebuild a global distribution network from the base set up prior to Pernod's distribution.

To stay alive, SPI/Stoli had to change how they did business. During this stressful and chaotic process the company challenged everything about their business. They realized that to be a successful global vodka brand, they could not continue to be so focused on "Russian-ness." So they changed. In 2008, the majority of management was from Russia. True, SPI/Stoli is still controlled by a Russian shareholder (living in the UK), but today the management team is as global as their market.

I asked the Russian woman sitting next to me in that bar in Hong Kong what she thought about the transition that SPI Stolichnaya had been going through the last few years from "Russian vodka" to "global vodka brand." She took my hand and said, "I love it! I have been with this company for decades, and we used to be so Russian. Now it is so different, so much better."

Some people will say that companies should not lose their connections to a country—that doing so will make them weaker. To make their point they usually bring up the example of "Swiss watches" or "Italian fashion brands, like Gucci." They say things like, "A quality watch has to be 'made in Switzerland.' Can you imagine a premium watch 'made in China'? That would be a joke." They say the same thing about the Gucci sunglasses: "Gucci sunglasses, made in Italy, says something about the quality of the product." Well, no, it doesn't. There are an estimated 200,000 Chinese migrant workers working in sweatshops *in Italy*. They work for "Chinese factories," located in Italy so that the factories can stamp "Made in Italy" on their products. The reason the quality of the Gucci sunglasses is so good is not because they are made in Italy, but because they are made by Luxottica, a sunglass producers, that, by the way, also produces sunglasses for Burberry, Chanel, Polo Ralph Lauren, Paul Smith, Stella McCartney, and virtually any other luxury brand that sticks their logo on a pair of premium shades. If Luxottica opened another factory in the U.S.—or in China, for that matter—using the same internal quality processes, they would still be Luxottica-produced sunglasses of great quality, right? Actually, Luxottica already has factories in America and China—as long as they are made by Luxottica, it doesn't matter if your sunglasses are made in Italy or China.

Which brings us to the Swiss watches. If a bunch of good-for-nothing uneducated bums from, say, Albania, moved to Zurich and started to produce watches of terrible quality they could still put "Made in Switzerland" on them. That statement says nothing about the quality of the watch. If you study the premium watch industry, you quickly realize that the crucial parts in all those luxury watches have been made by one company: Swatch. When it says "Made in Swizerland," it actually means "Made by Swatch." If Swatch opened another factory for watchmaking in, say, Albania, it would still be a great watch.

The image of an "Indian company" in the minds of most people is, unfortunately, corruption, red tape, and general ineffectiveness. Yet, Tata is a company founded in India, by the Tata family, generally considered to be a very honest, admirable and effective owner. So, is Tata an Indian company or the opposite of an Indian company? Answer: It is a company. Period. A company built on the strong values of its founding family, who still are active in running the group. The values of the founders were so strong that for decades they were not even written down. It was not until 1995 that then Group Chairman Ratan Tata decided to finally formalize the values and actually write them down. A first draft that he received read that the purpose of the Tata Group is "to improve the quality of life in India," but that was changed by Mr. Tata to "to improve the quality of life of the communities we serve."

Regardless if these communities are in India or not.

That means, for example, that Tata Technologies – headquartered in an affluent suburb of the metro Detroit area – supports community initiatives to help the less fortunate in areas fewer than 30 minutes from its North American headquarters. The name of the suburb? Pontiac, Michigan. Yes, the same Pontiac as the once great "American car company brand" with the same name.

So, here is an "Indian" company investing money and resources in a local community that is, quite literally, on the other side of the world. Why? Because Tata Technologies has more than 500 employees and dozens of key client organizations in metro Detroit and the company is built on the values of the Tata group, which include service to, and support of, the communities in which they are active.

One more example: On the back of the computer that I am using to write these words, it says "Designed by Apple in California. Assembled in China." I would argue that the "by Apple" is what makes an Apple product an Apple product. The "in California" part adds nothing to the quality of the product or to my perception of the product. The knee-jerk reaction for why Apple should keep the "in California" is to reply, "People like California and what it stands for," or "Apple was started in this garage in California so it shows their heritage." Fine, but how does that make the brand stronger for a buyer in, say, Indonesia, Poland, Germany, or India? Wouldn't the brand connect more closly to Mac users around the world if the back of the computer just said: "Designed by Apple."? The "Assembled in China" phrase, by the way, is only there because Apple has to put it there. But "Made in China" says nothing about the quality of a product. Some of the worst quality products in the world come from China, but Apple has moved the assembly to China because China is the only place in the world, at the moment, where Apple—famous for its addiction to quality—can get someone to assemble their products according to their high demands. You could argue that "Assembled in China" is actually a mark of world-class quality, since one of the most quality conscious companies in the world has chosen to lay its assembly there.

TAKE AWAY

What you do defines your character, not where you are from. Equally, your brand should stand for what you do, not where you do it. Does it? If not, is there a risk that your brand is not as closely connected to your products as it should be?

Notes

"Different Languages. One World. One company." LYRIC LABS INDIA PVT LTD

SAS: World Experts
It is a complex world.

SCENE: PHONE CONFERENCE BETWEEN LONDON AND THE USA

For many years, SAS seemed like two companies: SAS USA, run by the company's dynamic founder and CEO, James Goodnight, and SAS Outside the USA. When the company was founded in 1976, SAS decided to focus on the American market. When they opened offices outside the United States, those offices were run like franchises—given a lot of freedom and permission to create their own way of doings things. Staffed with locals, the overseas offices had limited collaboration with their U.S. counterpart. Obviously, the "two companies" would meet and share best practices, but they had different contracts, different invoicing, different management styles, and so forth.

About six years ago, this started to change. The company intentionally set about to merge the "two" SAS companies into one. Mikael Hagström, Executive Vice President of Europe, Middle East, Africa and Asia Pacific, who has been running the SAS non-American operations, had an important role in this transformation. With an office next door to James Goodnight, he has worked closely with the company's founder over the last few years to create "One SAS." I was able to book a phone interview with Mr. Hagström to find out what prompted this change.

BACKGROUND

"The world's problems are becoming more complex," Mr. Hagström said. "Today's supply chains, for example, are global. When there is a flooding in Thailand, Silicon Valley runs out of silicon. And since we work with supply chain optimization, we have to understand this new world. Before, you could have one person at a [client's] HQ who was your contact person, and we could just talk to him. Now everything is more complex. Now we need to have contact with the guy at their HQ, and their factory in Thailand, talk to their experts who sit in Singapore, and so on."

He gave me other examples of how demands from customers pushed SAS to become "one" company. In one instance, SAS was asked how to handle risk management for nuclear power plants. Few countries have a market for an expert on nuclear power plant risk management, but when you treat the world as your market, it is suddenly possible for SAS to have a team to specialize on that - a team that is then utilized around the world.

In another instance, a global insurance group with 75 million customers in about 70 countries needed to make a significant investment in one standard analytics platform. With the high level of risk and volatility in today's markets, it was of the utmost importance that this group could act quickly and seamlessly to protect its investments and make the right decisions on behalf of their clients, who count on the fact that their pensions are secure. When this insurance group chose SAS as their worldwide standard for analytics, having consistency across borders while being able to deliver locally was essential.

As you can tell, SAS works on major problems, and these problems are now bigger and more complex than ever. "The decision making process has changed radically, and in some industries, like energy, this change [to a global market] happened very quickly," explained Mr. Hagström.

I asked him how this added complexity on a global stage had changed the way they ran SAS.

"Traditional management tools, like budgets, become almost meaningless, and a business plan can be radically changed [in a short period of time]. So instead, it becomes more important to give individual leaders control of what they do." Mr. Hagström continued, "The advantage of this is not only that you become faster, but you get a different kind of ownership when the person who comes up with an idea also is the person who gets to make it happen." Of course, the disadvantage carries a risk, or feeling, of loss of control from the top management. According to Mr. Hagström, letting go can create friction, but it is something that has to happen if you want to be able to innovate as fast as the market is changing. That includes giving people the freedom to make mistakes.

"In order to innovate, you have to allow that something goes overboard once in a while."

The interesting thing is that it is Mr. Hagström's experience that the freedom to fail creates a bigger commitment to success.

"People will be more dedicated [to solving a problem] if they have been responsible for something that went wrong."

Another way of saying it would be: We take responsibility for the things we are accountable for. In a complex and fast changing world, an organization needs more people to take responsibility for what they doing, instead of just waiting for someone to tell them what to do.

TAKE AWAY

In a macro world, micro-management will not work. How do you manage?

Notes

"One World. One Company. One Nnumber." PRISM POINTE TECHNOLOGIES, LLC

One World. One Company — But Not One Way
The power of pragmatism.

SCENE: A MEETING ROOM OVERLOOKING THE SINGAPORE STRAITS

The world of business is not always as simple as business books want it to appear. Reality is just not as black and white as the text in a book. And that is true also for this book. I am not trying to make you believe that there are only two types of companies: The truly global companies that are doing great, and the not truly global companies that are therefore not doing great. I am trying to explain what we can learn from some companies about what they are doing right (or wrong) so that we can all improve. But I am the first to sign up to the idea that there are no truths written in stone. And that is why it was so inspiring for me to sit down with Mr. Choo Chiau Beng, CEO of Keppel, and his management team, for an interview about how this 20 billion dollar company is looking at the concept of being One.

BACKGROUND

Keppel is a company that is not easy to categorize. It is the world leader in the offshore and marine market, but originated in a country (Singapore) that has no oil and natural resources at all. In the offshore and marine industry, they are a global player, but at the same time they are a very local player in the Singapore real estate business.

I sat down with Mr. Choo Chiau Beng to see what others could learn from a company that is so diverse in its operations and locations. I began with my usual question: If he saw his company as "global" or not. He replied, "We are a 'multi-local company.'" He then explained what he meant, "Take our offshore and marine market, for example. We had no choice but to become local. We had to compete with local players for business, since we did not have a home market for ourselves to fall back on." The oil and gas industry is a very emotional industry. The feeling from Keppel's customers can often be: "This is my oil (therefore) I want to use my own (local) people." To manage that, Keppel employs Brazilians in Brazil, Americans in the U.S., Indonesians in Indonesia, and so on, promoting themselves as "local" in each market.

In a pragmatic tone, Choo Chiau Beng explained, "We are local when they want us to be, and sometimes we are more local than the locals!" At the same time they are building a company of "Keppelites", the name that the employees of Keppel call themselves. So, while being very local towards their customers, behind the scenes they are working to become One. "You can be an Indonesian and still be a Keppelite, or a Brazilian, or a American or…" He thought for a while and added, "If you are human you can be a Keppelite!"

When I suggested that, to many, what he just had described might sound like contradictions, he stopped me, looked me in the eye, and said, "It is always Yin and Yang. In everything there is an opposite."

"But doesn't it create a lot of friction?" I objected.

He laughed and said, "It's not friction! It's the importance of duality!"

He then went on to tell me how this attitude of duality runs through the company. I learned how Keppel needed to balance their culture of integrity and openness with the tendency of employees in some countries to under-report safety statistics in order to not lose face. So how do you balance those two apparently opposite viewpoints? Pragmatism. By not punishing every concealed accident, they can work on slowly changing the culture in those countries.

Keppel even has duality in their values. For most companies, the values are sacred words that describe what the company stands for. But Keppel has different ways of describing the same value for their different entities. For Keppel Offshore & Marine, the value is "can do!" For Keppel Land, it is "Passion." Another value is "Teamwork" for Keppel Offshore & Marine, and "collective strength" for Keppel Corporation.

When I question how one company can have different words to describe themselves for different divisions, the Keppel CEO just replied, "We are not so hung up on the words." Which, when you think about it, makes total sense. The underlying meaning of the different values is the same. They have just been packaged in a way that make them more relevant to the different personalities that work in the different businesses. A pragmatic way of looking at how to create universal values for a company with divisions that are from different worlds.

I left the interview with Choo Chiau Beng with a refreshed appreciation for pragmatism. Pragmatism might just be one of the most undervalued things in business. To be pragmatic means to deal with things sensibly and realistically, in a way that is based on practical rather than theoretical considerations. As I hope you have understood by now, the purpose of this book is not to define One way to become a company of One. Instead, it is written as a collection of stories about how different companies of different sizes and backgrounds, and in different situations, have chosen to approach the concept of becoming a company of One.

TAKE AWAY

So the last take away of this book could be said to be the take away for how to use any message in the book you are now almost done reading: Be pragmatic. Use the advice that is practical for your business. Discard that which is not relevant. I am aware that not everything will have been of value for you, but hopefully you have received nuggets of useful information and I hope that the overall message of the book has inspired you to try to transform your own organization to a company of One.

Being Branchless

It is often said that a person without roots is fickle; she doesn't know how to connect to who she is, and she can be easily manipulated because there are no basic values keeping her grounded. Roots are important.

However, if one is going to use a metaphor (in this case of likening a human to a tree), one has to use the whole metaphor. It is equally true that a tree without branches dies as well.

A tree that is not spreading its branches in all directions to gather as much energy as possible might have deep and strong roots but will still wither and die.

In other words, to be rootless is dangerous, but so is being branchless.

If your own culture is the root system, cultures of the rest of the world are the energy your branches need to reach. In doing so, you can reap new ideas about how to do things by learning from others, be inspired to try new foods, form new habits, and create new traditions. It will allow you to exercise your curiosity about other ways of doing things and energize you by giving you alternative points of view. And that creates creativity.

This is as true for individuals as it is for organizations.

Summary

NOW WHAT?

A good book should make you think. A great book should make you take action. I hope that the stories in this book made you think differently about what you do, and consider how you and your organization could become more global and behave more as One. Now it is time to take action. Below is a summary of the different take aways in the book. Go through them again and make sure that your new ideas translate into things you will do to change. As the saying goes, actions speak louder than words.

Speak "Bad English." Better yet, preach it!

Sharpen your recruitment process to get people with the same values instead of the same nationalities.

Increase your cross-border communication to get a better understanding of what happens in the world.

Stop thinking in terms of "export" and "markets," and start thinking about selling and helping customers.

Identify the best people in the world on the subjects that are most relevant to you - then contact them and use them.

Be aware of how a changing market might create new global competitors.

Build your brand around who you are and what you do — not where you are from.

Travel more to get fresh ideas, new perspectives and different viewpoints.

Make sure your organization is becoming global, not just your operations.

Use the vast resources in the world to make your own product and services the best they can possibly be.

Let the main office focus on strengthening the core values of the company, not just on collecting endless amounts of information. Less brain, more heart.

Beware of the ignorance that breeds when there is no curiosity about the outside world.

Create processes to better harness the competence in your organization, to make sure that the best people get promoted, regardless where they happen to be sitting.

Take advantage of the huge opportunities that borderless thinking brings.

Be prepared to challenge how you look at your market, and to start thinking in broader terms.

Realize that inspiration comes from getting new insights and new perspectives.

Expand the pool of potential persons you look for when you recruit.

Challenge any internal process that is hindering you from research at your full potential.

Encourage best practices to spread around the whole organization.

Learn to take advantage of how all the new tools make it easier to work as One.

Don't use the excuse of being too small to stop you from trying to become more global in the way you do business.

When you add new companies or entities, be sure to do so in a way that fully takes advantage of the competence coming into the new organization.

How is changing customer behavior changing how you should sell and distribute your products and services?

If you put country origin into your company description, you better have a very good reason for it—otherwise, drop it.

Become more human by being less nationalistic.

Be sure that your procedures are helping you become One—not stopping you.

Never stop looking for the next development around becoming One; the world never stops changing.

Look out for how your industry might be rewritten as a new, global player emerges.

Organize yourself in a way that different ideas from different people from different backgrounds join the debate about which of different ways would be the best.

Think about the basic human need that you could be solving and your potential market expands.

Embrace "Facebookism"—increase connections between people, break down barriers, and help small teams work on their projects in a decentralized, diverse, and free way.

Practice Pragmatism.

Acknowledge that leadership can be not only about the big things; it sometimes comes down to the small but symbolic ways you do things.

Understand that your brand has to be about you, not the country where your company was founded. They are two totally different things.

Trust in the competence of your staff and let them be as free as possible—but not freer.

And finally, as with anything else: Have fun, be honest, and do the best you can.

Final Words

In software development, it is common to invite early adopters to try the program out before it is officially launched to get suggestions on improvements, find errors that need to be fixed and get valuable input from the market.

We thought, why not use the same idea for a business book?

More than 2,500 copies of an early version were bought by companies who wanted to help make the book as good as possible because they believed in the theme of *One World. One Company*. Hundreds of other people downloaded a free beta version online to help make the book better.

I am very grateful for all the ideas, suggestions—big and small—that I got from the "beta-readers."

But perhaps the most valuable insight for me was the effect the book had on the readers. Some "got" the message after a few stories; some wanted more stories about more companies. But almost everyone agreed that the most valuable lesson they got from the book was the insight about what it means to have a "global mindset."

And that has also been the main purpose for me in writing this book. A global mindset gives us a more open, diverse and humble way of looking at the world. It makes us look at the bigger picture; it helps us see further than our own little group. It makes us want to learn from everyone and inspires us to try to be the best in world. And in the end, I think, it makes us more human.

Remember, global business is not The Olympics—it is Formula One racing. Global business is not a group of companies from different countries competing against other companies from other countries. Rather, just as in Formula One racing, it is a series of companies that acquire the best people, resources and suppliers that they can find in the world, to compete against other companies which acquire the best people, resources and suppliers from around the world.

The Ferrari F1 team has a Spanish and a Brazilian driver, and are sponsored by "Dutch" Shell, "Taiwanese" Acer, as well as from Mubadala Development Company (an investment company owned by the Emirate of Abu Dhabi), which also owned five percent of Ferrari shares as of the 2007 season. A global mix of competencies endeavoring to be the best.

Are you looking at the world of business as The Olympics or as Formula One?

What did You *think?*

This is where this book ends. But the communication continues. We would love to hear the comments, thoughts and ideas you have now, after having read the book.

Please send them directly to the author at: *fredrik.haren@interesting.org*.

If you tweet, blog or write about the book, we would also love to know. Include *@fredrikharen* in your tweets and send an email to *fredrik.haren@interesting.org* with a link to what you have written.

If you like the book, we would very much appreciate if you would write a review on Amazon.com.

Thank you.

Notes

"One Sim One World One Company" ROAM1 MOBILE SIM

Notes

Notes

"One World, One Company" CRABTREE OF GATESHEAD

Notes

"One world. one company" CYNOSURE

Notes

Notes

"One world, one company" MOLEX

Notes

"One World, One Company" WABROKER

Notes

OTHER BOOKS BY FREDRIK HÄRÉN:

The Idea Book

The Idea Book has sold more than 200,000 copies around the world, and has been translated into fifteen languages. The book was so popular in Iceland that 3,000 copies were sold in a month—meaning that it only took 30 days for 1 % of Iceland's population to come in contact with the book!

The Idea Book was recently included in the American book *"The 100 Best Business Books of all Time"* by Jack Covert and Todd Sattersten.

Find out more about *The Idea Book* at: *www.TheIdeaBook.org*.

The Developing World

How an explosion of creativity from developing countries is changing the world—and why the developed world need to start paying attention.

There is an explosion of creativity happening in the developing world right now. Best-selling creativity author and keynote speaker Fredrik Härén wanted to understand what this creativity explosion means, what it will lead to and how it will change the world.

So he set out to find out.

For five years Fredrik Härén traveled to 18 developing countries (and eight developed countries) and conducted more than 200 interviews with people who are in some way involved with business and creativity.

He met with cosmetics executives in Russia, professors in South Africa, creativity consultants in Egypt, IT journalists in Iran, hotel managers in Dubai, designers in Indonesia, government officials in Thailand, mobile phone designers in South Korea, and many more.

The result of his research is the book *"The Developing World."*

In this book you will learn about the advantages of being a creative person in a developing country, about what the developed world can learn from the developing world, and, most importantly, you will read about the dangers of defining yourself as "developed" in a world that has never been developing faster than now.

It is a book that may turn your view of the world upside-down, and hopefully inspire you to become more curious about the great changes happening in the world right now.

Find out more about the book at:
www.TheDevelopingWorld.com

Thank You!

First of all, from the bottom of my heart, I wish to extend a big thank you to my wife, Elaine. Without your love and support, I never would have been able to complete this book. But more importantly, life would be much less beautiful. You make me a better person.

I would also like to thank the following people for their fundamental help with making this book so much better:

Teo Härén	Phil Libin
Berit Härén	David Mayo
Torbjörn Härén	Tim Pinnegar
André Wognum	John Thuestad
Bastian Döhling	Mattias Miksche
Andrew Vine	Petter Andersson
Sara Herrlin	Greg Brooks
Sanna Rudling	Aðalsteinn Leifsson
Mikael Wanland	Peter Sund
Rikard Steiber	Peter Lundahl
Tom Johnstone	Michael Andrews
Johan Stael Von Holstein	Nick Emery
Mikael Pawlo	Mikael Hagström
Johan Ronnestam	Dale Steichen
Rachel Campbell	Björn Naglestad
Peter Vesterbacka	Madan Nagaldinne
Simon Dale	Nicolas von Rosty
Joerg Dohmen	Charles Doyle
Peter Baker	Diane Ho

Elizabeth Portiz Tamano
Dimitrios Karras
Evangeline Davis
Allen Perez
Ivaturi Vijaya Kumar
Kasie Abone
Gustaf Antell
Eiler Fagraklett
Tanupriya Anand
Jens Skov
Ana Filipa de Oliveira Ramos
Marcelo Tripoli
Richard Bleasdale
Marko Klijn
Pat Sloan
Emin Guluzade
Nick Emery
Cristina Blanaru
Hana Haatainen Caye
Helena Fagerström

Becky Mew
David Walker
Anika Desai
Audrey Tok
Niklas Olsson
Chatarina Schneider
Ayachana Hettiarachchi
Ashutosh Srivastava
Antonio Hidalgo
Choo Chiau Beng
Gordon Coburn
Georgette Kolkman
Patrick McGoldrick
Marco Ferrari
Brant Long
Audrey Gan
Sandra Aung
G-third atanque
Mary van Bronkhorst

… and everyone else who helped with making this book become a reality, including all the "beta-readers" of the first drafts of this book.

An extra big thank you to everyone at Mindshare for supporting this project and making it happen.

Finally, a huge thank you to all the amazing clients of interesting.org who made it possible for me work with, and learn from, some of the most interesting companies in the world. You inspire me.

Tell a Friend

Ideas are there to be passed on! Do you know someone who would or should buy large quantities of this book? Then do this:

1. Send an email to the person in question and recommend this book. (Tell them about: *www.interesting.org/owoc* too!)

2. Send a copy of your email to: *fredrik.haren@interesting.org*.

For Your Company

If you are interested in placing bulk orders of this book to inspire the staff of your organization and to get them to see the advantage of becoming a truly global company, please send an e-mail to: *info@interesting.org*.

Book a Speech or Workshop

Invite your coworkers or customers to an inspiring seminar by a world-class speaker. Fredrik's style of speaking is an unique mix of content and entertainment, inspiring and thought provoking at the same time.

His main topics are Business Creativity, change, and global business.

Fredrik has been invited to speak in 45 countries. Satisfied customers include IBM, The Swedish Parliament, The Singapore Police Force, Hewlett Packard, China Mobile, Ogilvy, American Express and hundreds of other clients in virtually all industries.

Some of Fredrik's awards include "Speaker of The Year" in Sweden and "Sweden´s ten most sought-after B2B speakers." He is based in Singapore but travels the world to speak.

About the Author

Fredrik Härén is an author and speaker on creativity and business. Over the last ten years, he has delivered well over 1,500 speeches at companies and organizations in virtually every industry; from nuclear power plants in Sweden, the Air Force in Sri Lanka, advertising executives in India, bankers in the United States, telecom managers in China, and many, many more.

His books have been translated into 15 languages and *The Idea Book* was included in *"The 100 Best Business Books of All Time."* This is his ninth book.

Fredrik is a true citizen of the world who has been invited to speak in over 45 countries on five continents. When he is not traveling, he splits his time between three countries. He is based primarily in Singapore where he lives eight months of the year with his wife and son. But the family also spends two months per year on his private island outside Stockholm in Sweden and another two months per year in Palawan, Philippines.

Fredrik is also the founder of creativity company, interesting.org, that he runs together with his twin brother Teo Härén. interesting.org is itself a global company. Teo lives in Älvkarleby, Sweden, the company's designer is based in Mariefred, Sweden, their programmers in Chennai, India, their 3D-animator in Manila, Philippines, their accountant in Singapore, and the proofreader for this book, Mary van Bronkhorst, is based in the United States.

The company has printers, publishing partners and other collaborators around the world. interesting.org sells its creativity speeches, workshops and books to clients in over 60 countries, from Iran to the U.S., from South Africa to South Korea, from Russia to the Maldives, from Chile to China.

In one sense, interesting.org is a company of just four employees; in another sense, interesting.org is a global company selling its products and services to clients worldwide.

During the last six years, Fredrik has traveled extensively to work with hundreds of organizations around the world. It is during his travels that the interviews, examples and stories for this book were collected. Most of the book was written in hotel rooms, Starbucks cafés, and on Ideas Island.

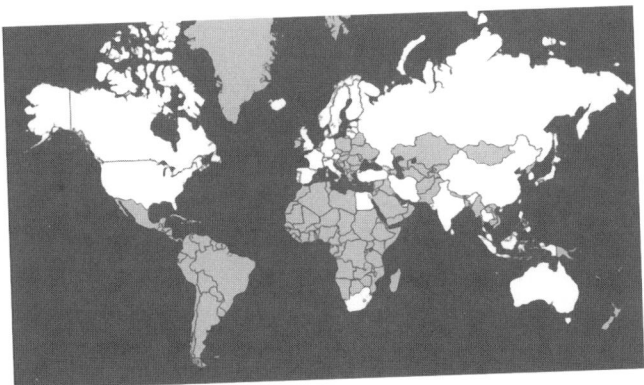

Fredrik Härén has been invited to work in the following countries:

Sweden	Lithuania	Turkey	Malaysia	Australia
Norway	Holland	Egypt	Indonesia	Taiwan
Denmark	Luxembourg	South Africa	Italy	Maldives
Finland	Germany	U.A.E.	Philippines	U.K.
Iceland	France	Iran	China	Cambodia
Russia	Austria	India	South Korea	Malta
Georgia	Switzerland	Sri Lanka	Japan	Ukraine
Estonia	Slovenia	Thailand	U.S.A.	Pakistan
Latvia	Monaco	Singapore	Canada	Macau

www.interesting.org/owoc

The book's own web site.

"One World, One Company" JAS HOLDINGS LTD.

Watch a 20 minute speech on the theme of this book at:
www.interesting.org/owoc.

"One World, One Company" KLIPSCH GROUP, INC.

"One World One Company" LTV

"One world, one company" MAPEI